Let's Enjoy Nature

Let's Enjoy Nature

A BOOK TO HELP PARENTS AND THEIR CHILDREN GET IN TOUCH WITH NATURE AND TO CARE FOR THE PLANET

Mildred Masheder

Cover Design and Illustrations by
Susanna Vermaase

GREEN
PRINT

First published in 1994 by
Green Print
an imprint of the Merlin Press Ltd
10 Malden Road, London NW5 3HR

97   96   95   94
5   4   3   2   1

ISBN 1 85425 084 1

Typeset by Stanford DTP Services, Milton Keynes
Printed in the EC by the Cromwell Press, Broughton Gifford

To Harry

Contents

Introduction

Are there days in your childhood that stand out in your memory: a family picnic in the woods, where you climbed the trees; a seaside holiday where you immersed yourself in sand; a birthday treasure hunt where you went chasing all over the common? Other memories might be more fleeting: kicking through autumn leaves to find conkers; blackberrying expeditions when you ate more than you put in the basket; making an enormous snowman with your fingers blue with cold; lying in a meadow full of moon daisies and poppies.

It was not so long ago that children could wander freely in much of the countryside; nowadays the restrictions are daunting: almost all of the meadows have been taken over by large scale agriculture; footpaths have become overgrown and cordoned off by landowners and trespassing is rapidly becoming a deterrent to anyone who wants to enjoy the open countryside. As children we would chant triumphantly, 'Trespassers can't be prosecuted!', because we had been told that 'they' would have to prove damage. Unfortunately this is no longer the case with regard to private property, which now covers most of the countryside; we can in fact be ordered off at any time, although trespass itself is not listed as a criminal offence at the present time. There is also the problem of security: parents feel rightly that if their children want to experience the real country, or even the commons and parks, that they should accompany them. If they can make time for this, it has its advantages and many of the open air activities in this book can be jointly shared, which is one of its main objectives.

But let us not despair, remember that, 'While there's a will there's a way', and this especially applies to keeping the footpaths open, a mammoth task pioneered by the Ramblers' Association; wasteland can be made into 'wildlife' land with the co-operation of the local community and there are hundreds of nature reserves and trails springing up all over the country.

What of our children? Have computer games and television taken over from mother nature? Certainly the electronic world has an immense attraction for children of all ages, often to the point of addiction; and this is greatly fortified by peer group pressure. As parents we are often uneasy about the influence of so much passivity, as our children become glued to increasing doses of violence and brutality. The question is how to prevent or counter habits that rapidly become ingrained and how to initiate more creatively active pursuits?

Fortunately there are two factors that act in our favour: one is the inborn fascination that young children have for the natural world. You have only to see them gazing fixedly at the motions of a fuzzy caterpillar; puffing at a dandelion clock; running their fingers through a rippling stream (or just the tap); concocting mud pies decorated with colourful berries, to know that this is their heritage. Their love of living creatures will continue throughout childhood if they have the opportunity to be in close contact with them and to care for them. The dilemma for parents is how to nurture these spontaneous inclinations when their children are growing up, so that they do not lose touch with the living world.

The second factor in our favour is the overwhelming propensity that all children have to be active – to be doing something at all costs – and the essence of this book is its concentration on activities, giving parents a host of suggestions that will help to bring their children into closer touch with nature. The hope is that if the ideas are stimulating enough, this will help to lure them away from the flashing lights and also to give them a sense of personal achievement. I should make it clear at this stage that this is not a direct attack on television for children; there are many worthwhile programmes for them to view, especially the superb nature series; it is a question of balance; how much they view and the content, and this is also the case with computer games.

So 'Let's Enjoy Nature' has as its main theme, as its title suggests, to appreciate in an active way the wonders and harmony of the natural world. Inseparable from this is the growing awareness of what mankind is doing to destroy the environment and to realise that adults and children alike need to play their part in helping to conserve it.

Although the book is mainly directed at parents, youth club leaders and teachers will find a host of ideas for activities that they can try out, both in their sessions and in co-operation with the parents of the children they are dealing with.

The book is divided into eight chapters, beginning with

NATURE IN THE HOME.   Chapter I
This chapter focuses on making the home an attractive nature centre, where children can have success in planting all kinds of pips, seeds and bulbs, where a variety of miniature gardens can be cultivated and where animals can be cared for, both family pets and 'short stay' creatures.

CONSERVATION IN THE HOME.   Chapter II
Here are ideas for saving energy in every possible way and also concentrating on the four RE's: refuse, re-use, return and recycle. Green shopping deals with how to avoid the plethora of polluting materials often used in washing and cleaning and on buying healthy alternatives.

MAKING THINGS FROM NATURE.   Chapter III
Children can explore natural materials such as clay, plaster and wood, making models of creatures and landscapes. They can use recycled items for sculpture and print in different media. They can experience free creativity as well as making presents from natural sources.

GARDENS FOR CHILDREN.   Chapter IV
You don't have to have a garden to enjoy planting flowers and
vegetables out of doors or to entice the birds. If you do have some
space then wildlife can be catered for and organic gardening can
be explored with the encouragement of environmentally friendly
creatures.

EXPLORING THE ELEMENTS.   Chapter V
This chapter provides challenging experiments with the basic
elements of earth, air, fire and water; the sun and the night sky,
and also the weather. It also gives ideas on how children can
test out the amount of pollution in the air and the water courses.

ENJOYING NATURE IN THE WIDER WORLD.   Chapter VI
Here is an invitation to venture out into the wider world of parks,
commons and the open countryside with family outings and
explorations. There is a special focus on the attraction that
children have towards woodlands, streams and ponds and the
seaside. It also gives information about the environmental
organisations that have a special section for young people such
as Watch, which is the junior wing of the Royal Society for
Nature Conservation and the Young Ornithologists' Club,
within the Royal Society for the Protection of Birds.

NATURE GAMES.   Chapter VII
These are a series of games all featuring nature; some are played
indoors but most of them are sited out to be enjoyed in the
garden, the parks or as a part of expeditions to the open countryside. There are old favourites adapted to a nature theme
such as treasure hunts and chasing games; others have a distinct
ecological basis: for example, litter hunts and food chain exercises.
All of these games are co-operative rather than competitive,
which is particularly valuable in a family context. All of the games
are equally suitable for families and clubs and camping, country
and seaside holidays.

CELEBRATIONS AND ACTIONS.   Chapter VIII
This is a calendar relating the established celebrations to the
seasonal cycles and including new festivals, specially created
to care for the environment. There are ideas for action and
pressure as well as the fun of celebrating events in the
community. There is emphasis on the connections with nature
in all of the traditional festivities and imaginative innovations
for the new ones concerned with conservation. Children are very
well aware of the dangers besetting the planet and many of them
will welcome the possibility of doing something about it, particularly if it is a joint effort with the school or the community.

No-one will want to attempt all of the activities described in this
book, but there is enough choice to satisfy the interests of most
families and clubs. As the emphasis throughout is on making
things rather than buying them, and experimenting with recycled
materials, this approach is not only ecologically sound but also
economically rewarding! Expenditure on heating and lighting
in the home can be reduced as can the shopping list and recycling,
re-using and refusing can become a way of life! I must add that
I myself am far from this ecological ideal, but in writing the book
I have become much more aware of the possibilities that I can
manage.
    A word about the role of the children: there is no indication
of the age range for the various activities, as families and clubs
will be in a better position to know what is feasible and what
would appeal to their children. When there is a wide age range
in a family, the older ones can sometimes set up suitable pursuits
for the younger ones. If there is an incentive towards action in
protecting the natural world, it may be that the older ones take
the initiative: a dramatic production about the rain forests, or
elephants being hunted for their tusks; an anti-litter campaign
or a sponsored walk for the RSPCA. It is very likely that the
younger ones will also want to participate and will be roped in;
in fact we should not underestimate the abilities of even quite
young children to take part in and even give the lead in conservation issues.

Children can make up their own code of practice, but it could contain such rules as leaving everything and every creature as you found it, (except in the case of litter!); never uprooting wild plants and only picking the flowers that you have grown, and caring for all wildlife, and lastly playing your part in making the planet a less polluted and a pleasanter place to live in.

An extra bonus for parents when their children get into the many activities described in this book is that they will provide a solid foundation for the work done in schools, especially with regard to the National Curriculum Science attainment targets. Home and School need to work together in all aspects of the children's learning as well as having a joint policy on conservation. A very practical way in which parents can support their children's interest in nature is to give them the tools to study it. If they are already fascinated by the natural world, a large magnifying glass will be a welcome present and later on they might look forward to a pair of binoculars or even a microscope as a special joint family present and this could prove to be an invaluable investment. Many future naturalists have started in this way. Family participation in the excellent nature programmes on television could also be an inspiration to follow up with exploration and field work on a local scale.

Chapter I

Nature in the Home

These first affections
are still the fountain light
of all our lives
William Wordsworth

It is in the home where our first affections are established and nurtured; not only our affections towards our family, but also everything that is part of our early experiences.

If the house is alive with flowers and all sorts of plants are being cared for, this is the starting point of a growing relationship with nature. There can be a blaze of colour all the year round: bulbs in the winter; buds blossoming in the spring; flowers in the summer and autumn leaves in the autumn.

Growing Bulbs in the Home   Bulbs for Christmas should be planted in September and kept moist in a cool, dark place until the shoots are well established. They are then introduced gradually to the light and watered sparingly. Crocuses can be grown in pebbles and hyacinths in water, but the usual mixture is some kind of fibre with potting soil. Next year it is best to plant them in the garden or better still in some communal place where everyone can enjoy them. (Remember, though, to get permission from the appropriate authorities.) Children will take pride in tending their own pots of bulbs.

Growing an Amaryllis   Perhaps the most spectacular bulb is the Amaryllis, which is very easy for children to grow. They can be planted from October right through to the spring, dis-

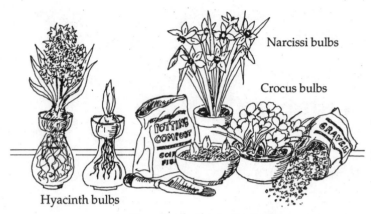

Narcissi bulbs

Crocus bulbs

Hyacinth bulbs

Growing bulbs in the home

playing a succession of colour throughout the winter. There is no need to buy expensive packages containing soil, a pot and the bulb, as long as you have good compost and potting soil. Just place the bulb with its roots in lukewarm water for 24 hours and plant it carefully in a pot so that its roots are not damaged, leaving half the bulb above the soil.

Keep the pot in a warm place, directly in the light and in a room temperature of about 20 degrees. What is miraculous is to see the stem shoot up and then the four-fold trumpets appear.

Amaryllis

Growing from Pips, Stones and Seeds

You can make your home full of fascinating plants: ones that you have grown yourself from seed or cuttings.

Successful Avocadoes Most of us have tried to grow avocadoes with tooth picks stuck in to balance them over a jar of water with the base just touching the water. It helps to soak them in warm water for a day or two and to peel off the thick outer skin. As long as you keep the water topped up, the roots should appear and when well established the plant can be transferred into potting compost, covering half the stone. I only knew of one person who actually raised a flower from an avocado stone, but it shows that it can be done!

Pipping We are inclined to give up if our seeds don't germinate, but if we persevere with lots of different species some will certainly succeed. Take pips from citrus fruits for example, they should be soaked for a day or two before being planted just under the potting mixture and stored in a warm, dark place for several weeks, keeping them moist by covering them with cling film. When two pairs of leaves appear, they can be uncovered and transplanted into little yoghurt pots with holes bored in the base and placed on a sunny window sill. So in this way you might be able to grow orange, lemon, tangerine and grapefruit plants, but don't expect any fruits! One useful tip is to choose the pips from a fruit that has plenty of them to spare.

Pipping

Peanuts   Have you ever thought of planting peanuts? Crack their shells and keep them in wet compost in a large pot on a warm radiator and when they have rooted and green leaves have appeared, they can be placed on a sunny window sill.

Begin a Date Palm   Plant fresh date stones in moist compost, cover with cling film or a plastic bag and leave them in a very warm place in the dark. Bring the plants out when the shoots sprout, but keep them inside the bags or cling film until they each have three leaves.

Start a Tree   As so many trees are disappearing it is a good idea to try to grow them from seed. The easiest to grow fairly quickly are conkers, acorns, beechnuts, also hornbeam and sycamore seeds. They should normally be kept outside during the winter in a tin pierced with holes in the base, but you could try keeping them in the fridge. Acorns and conkers can be made to sprout indoors on the top of a narrow necked jar with the root end just touching the water, or alternatively in compost on a sunny window sill with cling film over them. Whichever method you choose transfer them into a pot of compost once they have rooted and sprouted, and finally make arrangements for the permanent site of your tree.

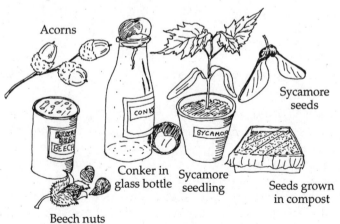

Acorns

Sycamore seeds

Conker in glass bottle

Sycamore seedling

Seeds grown in compost

Beech nuts

Start a tree

Fruit and Vegetable Tops   Most children have been successful in producing leaves from carrot, parsnip and turnip tops in saucers of water, but have they tried more tropical plants such as pineapples? The pineapple tops should be cut so that no fruit remains and then left on their sides for several days before planting in damp sand and kept in an airing cupboard or on a radiator, covered with a plastic bag or cling film. They can be transferred into pots when they have at least three leaves and kept on a sunny window sill.

Extra Sunshine   So much indoor planting success depends on a sunny window sill that extra sunshine is very welcome. Fix a reflector of tin foil or a mirror behind your seedlings so as to reflect the sunshine on them. Another idea is to hang a light to shine down on them so that they get extra sunshine hours.

New Plants from Old

Taking Cuttings   You may have geraniums, begonias or busy lizzies already in the house and you can make cuttings from them quite easily. Just cut a shoot about 4" long that has not flowered, above a joint so that the parent plant can produce a new shoot there. Then trim the cutting just below the next joint, remove the lower leaves, dip into hormone rooting powder and plant in sand or a mixture of half sand and half compost and cover with a plastic bag. Alternatively they can be kept in water in a jam jar until the roots are well formed and then transplanted. Philodendron, Coleus, Tradescantia and Peperonias are all suitable for taking cuttings.

New Plants from Leaves   It is fun to make new plants from leaves: you take begonia or African Violet leaves and trim the stem, leaving it about 1" long, and put them into compost or sand, or a mixture; or you can make cuts in the main veins and pin them down with hair pins. When the plants have rooted securely, they can be separated and transplanted. We all know that baby spider plants and mother of thousands can be cut off continually and potted, but not many people are aware that a head of the popular umbrella plant will take root if placed upside down in water. With Christmas Cactus you simply take off a string of leaves and plant it in fairly dry compost and sand, and water it sparingly with rain water. When possible it is always better to use rain water, although it is not now free from pollution.

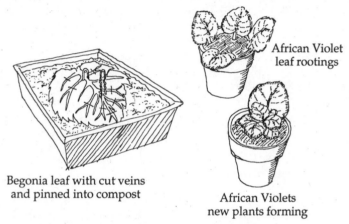

Begonia leaf with cut veins
and pinned into compost

African Violet
leaf rootings

African Violets
new plants forming

Propagating Cacti   This brings us to real cactuses; (Christmas cactus only being a succulent). These are the easiest of all to propagate; just take baby shoots off the top of any cactus and plant in sand, but you need to wear strong gloves. They will grow readily on a sunny window sill with no water until early spring, and then sparingly in the summer.

Babies from Bulbs   Daffodils, Narcissi and Tulips often produce small babies which can be broken off and grown for a new crop.

Bulblets from daffodil bulb

Miniature Gardens

If you haven't got an outside garden, you can always have an inside one. Here are a few ideas on the miniature gardens you could make:

Your Model Garden   This could be your dream garden or a plan of your own special plot outside. Fill an old roasting tin with charcoal and pieces of pot for drainage and cover with potting soil. Now have fun planning the layout: it could have a tiny lawn made out of a small piece of fine turf, or it could be planted with grass seeds and cut with scissors. Then you could make little pathways, a tiny rockery with alpine plants and borders, dwarf versions of herbaceous plants such as cyclamen and even a miniature rosebush. When the plants get too big, they can always be transplanted into separate pots. The important rule is to make sure your miniature garden does not dry out and is given regular feeding.

Miniature Bulb Gardens   These can be entirely made up of attractive pebbles with purple or white crocuses, scillas, snowdrops and grape hyacinths inserted amongst the pebbles. Remember that they need a long period of being kept slightly moist in a cool dark place before bringing out into the daylight when they start to shoot.

Bottle Gardens   These are great fun to make and require little attention, as condensation provides the watering. You can sometimes get large sweet bottles from shops and these are ideal; they can be upright or laid on their sides. Place charcoal on the base and fill one-third of the bottle with compost. Plan the layout of your garden with tall plants at the back and creepers over the floor. Plants to include could be: pansies, prayer plant, maidenhair fern, tradescantia, coleus and spider plant. You will need long tools to plant them, especially if you decide to keep the bottle upright; although if the children's hands are small, they can reach in to do the planting. Otherwise tie thin bamboo canes on to old spoons and forks and also to sponges to serve as tools for planting and cleaning the sides of the bottle. Use a cotton reel on a stick to press the plants down firmly in the compost, which should be thoroughly damp. Then no watering is needed as long as the bottle is fitted with a stopper, because the leaves provide condensation. Keep your bottle in a light place but avoid direct sunlight.

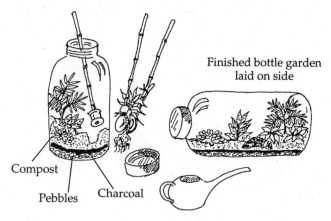

Finished bottle garden laid on side

Compost

Pebbles   Charcoal

A Miniature Woodland Garden   Bottle gardens are ideal for woodland scenes with rocks and small logs covered with moss, and, transplanted (from your garden), snowdrops, primroses, wild anemones and bluebells, giving a micro-impression of a spring wood.

A Miniature Desert Garden   Use a large earthenware saucer, line it with gravel and then a mixture of equal quantities of coarse sand, potting soil and compost, with small rocks artistically placed. Plant a whole variety of cactus seeds, bought from a seed merchant or good nursery, and water them very sparingly and wait patiently for them to appear. Alternatively get friends to give you baby shoots from their cacti and they will root and grow much more quickly. In both cases you must keep the seeds and shoots very warm. Make your desert garden an oasis with fine sand round a small mirror or a piece of glass with blue paper underneath, with model palm trees made of plasticine surrounding it.

A miniature desert garden

Insects in the Home Have a cage ready for insects you want to bring home for a few days; it can be made out of a clear plastic container with muslin covering the top, or a close wire mesh cylinder with round cake tins for the base and the lid as shown in the illustration.

Wire mesh cylinder with round cake tins for base and lid

Plastic container with muslin top

Keeping Caterpillars If caterpillars are your guests in the insect cage they will need fresh sprigs of their favourite leaves daily in a small jar of water with the top plugged with cotton wool so that they don't fall in and drown. They split their skin several times before they turn into pupae (or chrysalides). A secure twig is needed for them to hang on to keep them cool. When the adult butterflies or moths emerge they will want nectar, so release them near some flowers.

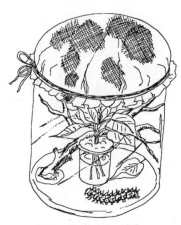

Keeping caterpillars

Keeping Stick Insects   Stick insects usually stick to privet in every sense of the word and they like a fresh supply every week. They lay tiny eggs, about 1 millimetre long, which are brown with a little yellow cap, and if you want them to hatch they will be really long-term visitors, as it takes six months (in a separate container).

Keeping a Spider   This should be a very short stay in the wire mesh cylindrical cage, with branches for webs fixed in the base with plaster of Paris. A wet sponge will provide moisture and tiny bits of meat or mealy worms to eat.

Keeping Pets

Can We Have a Pet?

The answer is another question: 'Will you be able to look after it yourself?' Just like us they need food, water, warmth, a clean home and attention and affection. This is often a tall order for young children and one solution is to have a family pet with everyone taking turns to look after it. There are far too many rabbits, hamsters, gerbils and budgies that provide endless reproaches from parents and endless guilt feelings on the part of their 'owners'. We have to realise that children have difficulty in envisaging a fluffy kitten or a playful puppy growing up to be quite different entities. Cuddling a baby rabbit is a delight, but turning out in the cold to feed it every day is another matter, and hamsters don't want to play until after most children's bedtime and they can sometimes give nasty bites if startled.

Health risks also have to be considered: cats and dogs can increase the dangers of food poisoning, so extra care has to be taken to be sure to wash hands before eating and that small children do not touch the litter trays or even get licked by an affectionate pet. The faeces of dogs and cats can spread toxocariasis which can cause blindness in children, so owners have a responsibility to the community as well as their own families to ensure that their pets are well trained to defecate in the proper places.

A further word of warning is to avoid buying exotic pets unless you are absolutely sure that they have been bred in this country. So many creatures like parrots and various reptiles have been snatched from their habitats, often from the rainforests, adding to the general destruction and making more and more animals in danger of extinction. Even if this were ecologically sound, the pets themselves would be unhappy in a cold climate so different from their own.

Having put the negative side, keeping a pet can be very therapeutic: stroking a cat does more good to us than it does to the cat, however appreciative it may be. Most of all, children learn to care and nurture, and at the same time they learn their responsibilities as well as getting a great deal of pleasure from their pet.

The RSPCA gives much good advice about looking after pets and their slogan is that a pet is not just for Christmas, but for ever; in fact it is usually until they die, which can feel like for ever in children's minds. Indeed the first real experience of death for most children who have cherished pets is when their beloved cat, dog, or budgie dies. In a society where death is often remote from the home and is hushed up in front of the children, the grief over the death of a pet can be treated with great sympathy and understanding, with talk, reminiscences and ritual burial. This will help children to come to terms with the frightening idea of death and we can share together the acknowledgement that all life must eventually die.

Owing to housing restrictions many families cannot keep a dog or a cat but there is a wide variety of creatures that can be kept indoors or in a small yard. Gerbils are more fun for children than hamsters, as they are lively during the daytime; rabbits take a relatively small space for a hut outside, although they really like a run on the grass. There are plenty of instructions available for all of the popular pets, so this book will concentrate on creatures that are kept in the home for a short stay and then returned to the wild.

Making an Aquarium   Handy people in the family could make a simple aquarium, which would also serve as a vivarium when dry. You get five pieces of glass cut and join them with waterproof tape to make a rectangular container. Make a rectangular wooden frame to fit tightly around the bottom of the aquarium. For safety you could glue the tank to a thick board with aquarium cement. Put gravel at the bottom, add rocks of various shapes and sizes and plant some water weeds with the tallest plants at the back and some floating ones on the surface. A filter is useful to keep the water clean.

Stocking an Aquarium   Fill it with pond water which will provide some livestock and supplement it by pond dipping, making sure you include water snails to keep the aquarium clean. You can stock it with goldfish or minnows, gudgeons, freshwater shrimps, damsel fly nymphs, sticklebacks, freshwater mussels, caddis fly larvae and water spiders if the temperature is kept between 55^0–70^0F, but for tropical fish, such as guppies, you would need a heater to keep it at 70^0–100^0F.

A Seawater Aquarium   You need 3oz of salt to 1 gallon of water and a few grains each of potassium sulphate, magnesium sulphate and magnesium chloride. Put plenty of rocks for shelter and stock it with sea creatures: prawns, shrimps, sea anemones and starfish and rocks encrusted with mussels.

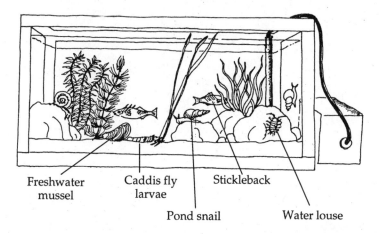

Freshwater mussel

Caddis fly larvae

Stickleback

Pond snail

Water louse

Setting Up A Vivarium You proceed as for an aquarium; place a shallow dish of water firmly in the soil and make sure that the top of the aquarium is securely covered with a perforated plastic sheet. Grow various plants in the soil making the habitat according to what your animal needs. For example, newts like a very damp environment with plenty of greenery. Terrapins need a mixture of part soil and rock, part water; they are fed on minute pieces of raw meat and fruit hung by a thread so as not to pollute the water. Slow worms like the damp and plenty of rocks to hide under. Slugs and snails like to eat many different kinds of leaves, but especially the ones near where they were found. You can see them eat with their saw-like tongues. They need a secure glass top on the vivarium to prevent them escaping. (When our pet newt went missing we found a horrible slimy smudge on the stairs!) Creatures needing a very damp atmosphere can have a small jar of water with a perforated cap to provide constant condensation as well as a very shallow saucer of water.

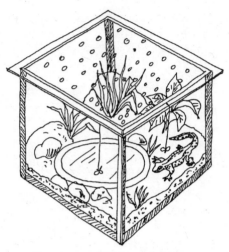

Keeping newts in a vivarium

Housing 'Creepy Crawlies'   A vivarium can be a very temporary home for creatures you have collected from leaf mould and decaying logs, such as woodlice, earwigs, beetles, centipedes and millipedes, but it needs to be covered with black paper as they are accustomed to the dark.

Making a Wormery   You put different layers of soil in a transparent plastic container, using sand, clay, chalk, loam etc. and topping it with dead leaves and small pieces of vegetable matter. It has to be kept dark with black paper covering it and the layers should always be moist. If the container is long and narrow, there is more opportunity of observing the activities of the worms, and, although it is more trouble, a really ideal viewing container is made from two rectangles of rigid plastic and one inch wide wood strips, assembled as shown in the illustration. This is the best way of showing the ripples the worms make in the layers and how they drag dead leaves down below. The children will collect the worms (we hope!) and apparently, if a fork is stuck down into the ground and banged, the worms will be curious enough to come nearer the surface.

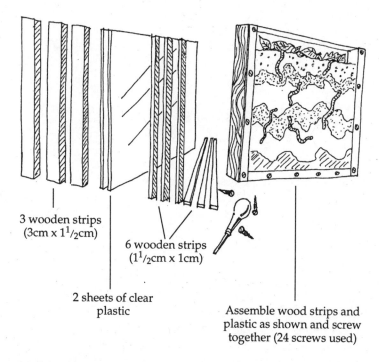

3 wooden strips
(3cm x 1$\frac{1}{2}$cm)

6 wooden strips
(1$\frac{1}{2}$cm x 1cm)

2 sheets of clear
plastic

Assemble wood strips and
plastic as shown and screw
together (24 screws used)

Making a Formicarium   You can use the same rectangular construction as for the wormery; this time filling the container with a layer of clay at the base and then with earth, making quite sure the top is securely closed! When you take a small section of ants from the antheap, you must be sure to include a queen (you can easily distinguish her as she is much bigger than the other ants), otherwise the ants will die in two weeks. If they are difficult to handle a short stay in the fridge (securely enclosed in a plastic bag!) will calm them down. Feed them with very tiny pieces of fruit and meat and a little honey and drops of water, and keep a wet sponge permanently on the top. When you have watched then constructing the tunnels and the queen laying her eggs, take them back to the antheap. (Can you imagine them telling the rest what happened to them – how there was an Ice Age?)

Chapter II

Conservation in the Home

Often families think that the problems of pollution are so immense that there is little they can do about it, and that their puny efforts to practise conservation in the home would be just a drop in the ocean. In fact if we were really careful not to use any toxic chemicals, it might be a purer drop that meets the ocean! Drops in the ocean from all the householders would make a tremendous difference to the well-being of planet earth, and if we maintain this care on every level of our daily activities much of the present pollution could be greatly reduced. It is true that industry has huge responsibilities to keep the environment clean; but if we are playing our part, then we shall be in a stronger position to challenge the captains of the industrial world to set their own houses in order!

Families could bear in mind the code letters: RE, which could stand for _Re_sponsibilities; _Re_fuse; _Re_-use; _Re_cycle.

Refuse Perhaps the most important of all is to refuse to belong to the 'throwaway' society, by refusing to buy goods that are not absolutely necessary. Like most of these recommendations there is an in-built bonus in refusing to buy in that it saves us a lot of money! We are all enormously pressurised to buy something new by the advertising media and this goes for our children too. It is hard for parents to resist their pleas to add to their collections of sets of toys or to exchange their last computer game for another, on payment of the fixed fee. Many of the toys on the market are eye-catching but shoddy and with a short life span, (unless you count the fact that most of them are made of plastic, so that they will outlive their owners a hundred times over in the refuse tips!).

Another way of refusing is to avoid unnecessary packaging, often with as many as three layers of plastic and paper. If enough people refused to buy these items, the manufacturers would soon keep packaging to a minimum. It would be cheaper for them to produce and this would surely be a plea which would reach their hearts!

Return   Sometimes you can get money for various bottles that you return to the shop; it means that glass, that takes power to make, can be used over and over again, so choose returnable bottles wherever possible. A few shops pay a small amount for plastic bags, which are sent to be recycled, alternatively customers bring their bags to use again. How many of us have a drawer so full of plastic bags that it is hard to open it? Some shops that sell cosmetics, like the Body Shop, have a system of refilling pots and bottles, which is a cheaper and ecologically sound practice.

Re-use   When we shop we can look out for items that we can re-use: for example, organic pump sprays for plants, which when empty can be filled with a mixture of soapy water to keep the pests down. Under the category of re-using comes the giving of clothes, utensils and toys to charity shops or having a car boot sale. Magazines are welcome at hospitals and nurseries as well as sturdy toys.

Recycle   Recycling is now a part of most people's lives: and the majority of activities in this book introduce the use of articles that otherwise would be dumped on the refuse heap. This applies especially to plastic goods that are only just beginning to be recycled industrially; meanwhile they are eminently suitable for growing plants, setting up experiments and for the children's constructive efforts.

Young children can have fun in separating the tins to be recycled and making sure that the aluminium ones, which are not attracted by a magnet, are put in a separate collecting box. It is best to deliver them already flattened and this should be a therapeutic occupation!

Recycle
separating aluminium tins with a magnet

Perhaps the most important item for us to recycle is paper and we are only too well aware of how many trees are being destroyed to cater for the demands of such a wasteful society. It stands to reason that we buy only recycled paper, which is now available from many stationers. We can re-use our old envelopes with sticky labels, which can also remind people of the need to conserve the trees.

Children often act as though paper grows on trees, which is sadly only too true; but one can still appreciate their art work at the same time as impressing on them the need to be economical with paper and to use both sides.

How Green is Your Home?

This chapter can remind us of some of the ways in which we can practise conservation in the home. These are mostly concerned with the saving of energy and the reduction of pollution and of course there is the added advantage of saving money at the same time.

Children as Waste Watchers   Children have been known to criticise their parents for wasting energy and material goods when they come home from school all inspired by lessons in conservation. They might take to the idea of being self-appointed waste watchers on a spot check basis on certain days chosen by them. They could devise a point system: plus 10 for something positive and minus 10 for something negative. This approach might not appeal to all families, but at least there is the advantage of drawing them in to face up to their own responsibilities for waste watching!

Waste Watchers in the Kitchen   If there is enough room for separate bins or boxes under the sink for tins, plastics and bottles this saves a lot of sorting afterwards, but most people have to be content with plastic bags waiting to be delivered to the banks. If children are able to collect them this would be a great service and they could make some pocket money at the same time, at least for the aluminium tins and returnable bottles and also perhaps from grateful householders. The biggest problem for most people is the storage and the delivery.

A waste paper basket in every room will help to conserve paper. It can be sorted to see what can be used for making paper and what can go to the paper bank, if necessary separating the cardboard from paper as not all banks take a mixture. Waste watchers might find paper thrown away which could have been used on both sides!

The most important refuse for the garden is the vegetable matter: peelings, cores, salad trimmings, tea leaves, leftovers (except meat). These can go into a strainer that is handy at the sink and then transferred to a container with some drainage and if possible to a compost heap outside. (See page 56.)

Waste watcher's
score card

Compost bin

Recycling
glass

Recycling
paper

Recycling
aluminium tins

Sink strainer for
vegetable matter

Bin Dip   Many of us mere mortals have not reached this fine art of sorting and if we are on the brink of thinking we will do something about it, a family game may be an inspiration! Wearing gloves, each member takes out one piece of rubbish from the bin and says what could be done with it. For example, many of the plastic containers have an infinite capacity for re-use, as is described in other chapters.

Energy Watching in the Kitchen   Boil only enough water for what is needed, rather than a full kettle for a cup of tea.

Keep the fridge door closed except for brief moments of opening. Set the thermostats of the fridge and freezer at a reasonable temperature.

Dishwashers can wait patiently for a full load.

Kitchen cloths (recycled) are more economical than rolls of kitchen paper.

Washing up under a running hot tap consumes much more energy than in the sink or a basin. (I have to confess that this is my continual temptation, which I do indulge in from time to time!)

Water Watching in the Kitchen   Use the bowl of rinsing water to water the plants.

Use water sparingly and turn off the tap when not in use.

We are told that there is now a permanent shortage of water, owing to greatly increased demand; this is sometimes hard to believe when the rain has been pelting down for days; nevertheless it is true that more reservoirs are always needed, so we can do our bit by economising on water whenever possible.

The following little exercise may bring home to children the fact that we take endless supplies of water for granted. It may give them an inkling of how so many people all over the world have to carry their water from great distances every day.

Water Rationing   Suppose you had to fetch your water from a well miles away and you could only carry a gallon. Could you manage to make this amount do for a whole hot day? The gallon would have to be the only drink, with concentrated juice added if necessary and it would have to last for washing and washing up, which of course children might be all too willing to skip! They might see how far they could carry a plastic container filled with a gallon of water; would it be easier to balance it on their heads? With what results!

Toxic Watch in the Kitchen   Environmentally friendly washing up liquid should be used and that as sparingly as possible. Toxic cleaners and bleaches do immense damage to our water courses with disastrous consequences to the soil and the wildlife. Use alternative cleaners like soda, vinegar and borax instead of toxic chemicals.

Water rationing

Waste Watching in the Bathroom   Showers are much more economical than baths, which can be more of a special treat.

Dripping taps need to be fixed promptly.

Toiletries can be environmentally friendly and not tested on animals.

Homemade herb bags for the bath can replace perfumed salts.

A brick or a weighted plastic bottle in the lavatory cistern can cut down the water used by half.

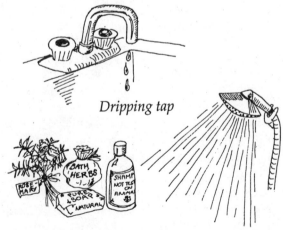

Dripping tap

Waste watching in the kitchen and bathroom

Waste Watching in the Living and Bedrooms   Thick curtains help to keep the cold out.

Draught excluders can be fixed to windows and doors.

Heating and lighting can be turned low or off when not needed.

An extra jumper can take the place of turning the heat up.

Long life electric bulbs are more economical.

Tape recorders and decks, etc can be plugged into the mains rather than using batteries, which contain toxic chemicals – battery chargers soon pay their way. (At this point I have to confess that my batteries expired on my electronic typewriter, which seems to be listening to what I write! I am now sold on buying a battery charger, not least to save money in the long run.)

Waste Watching in the Children's Rooms   Boxes can store items that can be recycled creatively: such as plastic bottles and containers; dressing up clothes and oddments for collage, including fabrics.

Waste watching in the children's room

Many of the points made are relevant to all the rooms but have not been repeated. More permanent items like furniture may be made of hardwood from the rainforests such as mahogany, ebony and rosewood and it is only when they are being replaced that sustainable timber can be chosen.

I should repeat that it is really difficult to maintain these standards of conservation in the home, but these points may help us to realise some of them.

Green Shopping   If you and the children can walk to local shops and save petrol, that means one less polluting car on the roads. It might be cheaper to buy in bulk from the supermarket, but it means that the children cannot easily take responsibility for the shopping, whereas they can go to local shops if it is safe. There is also the possibility of having fresher food if it is bought in small quantities and it is less likely to be wasted.

There is another advantage in walking to local shops. You are more able to be aware of the natural world as you go: finding a special treasure, looking at trees, hearing a bird song, seeing what can grow between the paving stones and in the crannies in the walls. There is a lot to explore even in the most built-up areas and with some encouragement children will respond to nature watching on the way to the shops or to school.

Green shopping

Shopping Rules

Overpackaging   The first golden rule is to take your bag or basket with you. The bag could be made at home out of hessian or similar strong fabric. You can then refuse extra wrapping with a polite, 'No thank you; I'm thinking about saving paper'. (I have had quite a good response to this approach, but I try not to be too self-righteous!)

Overpackaging
(string bag & shopping trolley)

Avoid over-packaged items as described under the heading of Refuse.

Try to buy goods in re-usable or returnable containers.

Think of pre-cycling: in other words buy goods that you know can later be recycled or, better still, returned for a deposit.

Avoid disposables, ranging from paper towels to razors, from ball point pens to plastic cutlery.

Never buy aerosol sprays and try to avoid pump sprays as they are too complicated to recycle.

Make sure that you do not buy any products made from some part of an endangered species, such as ivory from elephants' tusks, snake or crocodile skins. This also includes any product made from the destruction of the rainforests. In this context it is valid to ask where the beef from your beefburger has come from; although it is unlikely that the whole story of the clearing of the rainforests for cattle will emerge!

Ask for organically grown fruit and vegetables where possible; if there is sufficient demand, the prices will come down.

Chapter III

Making things from Nature

The inspiration for so much of our creativity lies in the beauty of Nature; and by making available natural materials of all kinds, we can provide a stimulus for our children's artistic ability, so that from an early age their creations are appreciated. They can begin to make things for themselves or for presents, starting with quite simple things like pot pourris and pomanders and progressing to beautiful handmade paper with motives of pressed flowers. They may well have some misgivings about competing with manufactured goods, but with encouragement and help in making gifts that are really acceptable, the pride in which they say, 'I made it myself' will enhance their confidence, and they will experience the joy in giving something of their own. It is important to stress however that the care and effort they put in to such finished products should not inhibit them from spontaneous creativity enjoyed solely for the pleasure in doing. Ideally the inspiration should be the mainstay, with increasing desire and ability to tackle the techniques as they grow older.

Making Animals

Modelling Animals in Clay Elephants and rhinos, both threatened species, stand solidly on their thick legs when made of clay. They need to be hollowed out before being fired in the kiln, or they can be made of grey clay and smoothed and polished with a spoon to look natural. The ivory tusks of elephants and the alleged potency of the rhino's horns have caused them to be slaughtered by the thousands by ruthless traders, so the models can be used for publicity to save them from near extinction. The time honoured way of modelling by hand is the coil method: rolling out long 'snakes', building them up into the shape desired and then smoothing them flat. Snakes and other reptiles can be rolled into thick coils and the heads and tails carved out.

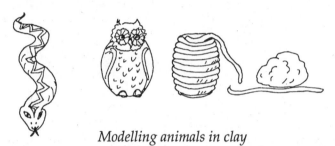

Modelling animals in clay

Cardboard Animals   Make a sketch of an animal on a piece of cardboard which is doubled, with the fold going along the back of the animal and continuing where the head will be. Fold a pleat to make the neck and head stand up from the back and fix it with a paper clip. Cut out the tail, legs and head through the double card, colour it and separate so that it stands on its four legs.

Animals Made of Cloth   Whales, seals, dolphins, moles and all sorts of furry animals can be cut out double from odd pieces of velvet or nylon, sewn together on the wrong side and then turned inside out and stuffed with pieces of old tights. Again most of these animals are under threat and the model can be used as publicity to save them.

Snake Doorstops   Sew a long 'sausage' of thick attractive material that would otherwise be thrown away; stuff it and use as a draught protector at the base of a door. This will be a great help in keeping the house warm and thus saving electricity.

Mobiles of Delicate Insects   Butterflies, moths, dragon and damsel flies can look realistic with painted tissue paper wings stretched on wire. They can also be made of delicate skeleton leaves cut out and painted.

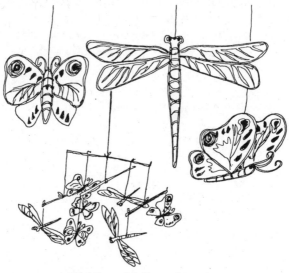

Mobiles of delicate insects

Papier Maché Animals   Use up your old newspapers by tearing them into small pieces and soaking them in water or wallpaper paste. Take an animal you have modelled in plasticine, spread it with vaseline and cover it with several coats of squeezed out papier mache, leaving each layer to dry before the next one. Then cut the model in two and ease the plasticine out and stick the two sides of the papier mache model together with glue and finally colour it and paint in the features.

Animals Carved Out of Plaster   This is an appropriate place to introduce plaster, which is child's play to make. Half fill an old plastic bowl with warm water and then gently sprinkle Plaster of Paris on it until it has absorbed so much that a peak of powder appears in the centre. Stir gently with your fingers to get the lumps out and give the bowl a few shakes to eliminate any air bubbles. The mixture, which should be of the consistency of thick cream, is then poured into a container such as a pint milk carton. After twenty minutes or so it will have hardened sufficiently to be able to peel off the surrounding card and then any creature can be carved out of it. If long bars of soap are obtainable, these are very satisfying to carve in the same way.

Animal Puppets   Children love making their own puppets and many animals are ideal as models. A puppet show with nothing more elaborate than a large cardboard box with the top and bottom removed, standing on a table, can be set up very easily. Elephants, rhinos, whales, dolphins, otters and owls can be cardboard cutouts held by a stick; crocodiles, snakes and seals can be made out of old stockings, painted or stuck with collages and fitted into children's arms with the hands being the mouthpiece. The choice of endangered species may be an inspiration for a theme on saving them!

Animal puppets

Leaf Printing

Leaf Pressing   Colourful patterns made by pressed leaves are great favourites pressed on to pads of foam, sponge or newspaper coated with different colours of either non-toxic printing ink, shoe polish, thick poster paints or gouache. With a little wallpaper paste, they can be printed on to paper or thin card to make creative decorations. A range of autumn colours can be specially evocative, and a mosaic of leaves can be used to decorate gift boxes and other models, and in this case the paint or ink would have to be permanent.

Leaf Pictures   This is an idea that older children can make for the younger ones. Take two rectangles of stiff cardboard of equal size, and make one into an open frame by cutting out a rectangle leaving a border all round. On the other card, stick a leaf, veins upwards, in the centre and stick transparent plastic over the whole card. Now sellotape the cards together so that the picture of the leaf appears in the centre of the frame. Young children can then rub coloured wax crayons over the whole picture on to a piece of white or coloured paper the same size as the card placed over the frame. This will produce a nicely framed picture. (Credit Hetty Kothari.)

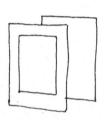  

Two rectangles of card. Cut a rectangle out of one to make a frame

Stick leaf on card and cover with cellophane. Stick two cards together

Cover leaf card with a sheet of paper. Rub over with crayon. Many rubbings can be taken

Leaf pictures

Leaf Silhouettes   Place some differently shaped leaves on a sheet of card and paint over them with large brush strokes so that when the leaves are removed there is a silhouette pattern left. You can then paint them choosing a different colour from the background. If the leaves are inclined to move, then secure them with a little glue, which will not show under the paint.

Vegetable Printing   Cut any of the following vegetables in half: potatoes, turnips, carrots, parsnips of different shapes and sizes. Dip them into thick non-toxic paint and press them down firmly onto white or coloured paper, making patterns of different colours with circles and ovals. The sizes can be varied by cutting the carrots and parsnips at intervals from the top to the bottom. Older children can carve a pattern on to the surfaces, making them deep enough to stand out from the base. They can paint on the colours with a brush and then print. These vegetable and fruit prints emphasise the symmetry and intricacy of all growing things and it is good to experiment with more unusual ones such as peppers and pineapples. The cut ends of the root vegetables can be 'recycled' by being used for sprouting in saucers of water.

Junk Printing   Lots of junk materials can be an inspiration to print: cotton reels, plastic containers, corks, string, grasses, twigs and lids (which have come off jam jars taken to the bottle bank). Mini prints can be made from half walnut, pistachio or peanut shells. A simple game would be to guess what objects have been used when a complex print is finished.

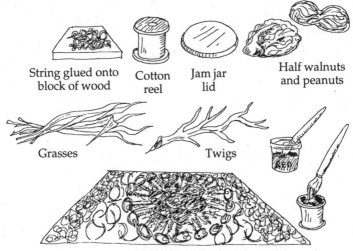

String glued onto block of wood

Cotton reel

Jam jar lid

Half walnuts and peanuts

Grasses

Twigs

Experimenting with mark making on paper or thin card

Junk printing

Hands and Feet Printing   Of course, the print makers that are always available are fingers, toes and feet, with lots of newspaper to protect the floor! This can be great fun if rigorously controlled, and the hands and feet of different members of the family can be combined to make harmonious patterns!

Invisible Footprints   Mix a teaspoon of baking powder in half a cup of water, wetting the foot with it, and then stand on white paper. To detect the footprints, warm the paper by holding it six inches above a candle flame (with adult supervision).

Invisible footprints

Guess the Animal   Use several layers of newspaper as inking pads with different coloured soluble inks or paints. Make pads for printing as described in Leaf Pressing (page 29) and use fingers or fists to paint animals in different colours. Can the others guess what animal it is?

Guess the animal

Collecting Things   There is a stage in their development when children are really keen on making collections; and there is enormous scope to be found in the realm of nature: shells are popular, as are different kinds of stones and of course the pressed flowers and leaves. I was the only one I knew who collected snail shells!

Stamp Collecting   There are numerous stamps that illustrate nature, such as birds, flowers and animals from the country of their origin. There are also stamps to campaign for the preservation of wildlife.

Make Your Own Notepaper   This activity will help children to treasure the value of the paper they use, especially when they endow their own notepaper with their logo or a delicate pressed flower.

The young ones can tear up white paper into tiny pieces and mix it with water to a thick paste. If newspaper is used it is best to bleach it in the sun, having sponged it with white vinegar or lemon juice. Never use bleach as it adds to the pollution, going down the drain and into the earth. Some people use a mixer for this initial process, but this takes away the satisfaction of doing it all by hand and not relying on electrical gadgets.

The next step is to pour the paste into a baking tin and to make a frame stapled with a fine nylon mesh. This could be an old picture frame, or four pieces of slatted wood, nailed to form a rectangle, or you could use the sort of flat sieve that is used to go over the gas ring. Then you 'fish' for the pulp by dragging the frame, nylon side up, just under the surface of the pulp and spreading it out evenly. When the water drains away it should be easy to turn the frame upside down on to a cloth and then to press it dry with another cloth on top. Then you can continue with further sheets of drained and pressed pulp, and when dry you can iron them and trim the edges and admire the texture of your newly created very own paper. If you prefer coloured paper, then a few drops of vegetable colouring can be added to the pulp before mixing.

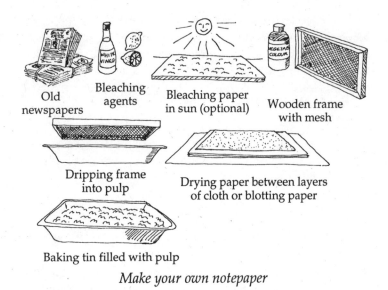

Old newspapers

Bleaching agents

Bleaching paper in sun (optional)

Wooden frame with mesh

Dripping frame into pulp

Drying paper between layers of cloth or blotting paper

Baking tin filled with pulp

Make your own notepaper

Pressing Flowers Flowers and leaves can be pressed between two sheets of absorbent paper and left under a pile of heavy books for at least two weeks. Then they can be placed face downwards on transparent book covering with adhesive backing and pressed down firmly. The transparent paper is turned over and pressed on to the card or object that is being decorated, or it can be stuck with egg white and covered with a prepared acetate sheet.

They can be used artistically in many ways: making pictures, decorating notepaper, book marks, waste paper baskets, etc. They can also be stuck onto windows, using clear plastic as a backing, sticking on the flowers with clear adhesive or egg white and covering them with a clear adhesive sheet. A window picture with patterns made of pressed flowers and leaves gives a wonderful translucent effect.

A Portable Flower Press With adult help cut two rectangles of plywood and drill a series of holes down the long side of each board and one hole in the corner of the other long side of each one. Cut several pieces of cardboard the same size as the plywood, punching holes to match the row of holes which will form the spine. Trim the corners of the card so that the corner holes in the plywood are free. Then bind the holes forming the spine of the book tightly with string and attach the remaining two corners to long bolts that have wing nuts. When each specimen is collected put it between newspaper and slip it into the cardboard pages of the press and tighten the bolts and leave for two or three weeks. Flowers, leaves and grasses can be pressed immediately on picking and have a better chance of being successful this way.

It is good to grow your own flowers to press, but if you do pick them from the wild, then only choose one and only if there are plenty more. Yellows seem to keep their colour better than most, but it is good to experiment; I found that purples could be very effective. Some enthusiasts press each petal separately and then have fun re-assembling them or making patterns for decorations on papier maché creations.

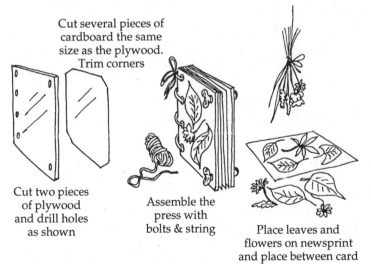

Cut several pieces of cardboard the same size as the plywood. Trim corners

Cut two pieces of plywood and drill holes as shown

Assemble the press with bolts & string

Place leaves and flowers on newsprint and place between card

A portable flower press

Pot Pourri   All sorts of sweet smelling ingredients can be dried and made into a fragrant pot pourri: rose petals, lavender, tiny pine cones, lemon verbena, orange and lemon peel with ground orris root from the chemist to make it last. Add various spices such as cinnamon, nutmeg or allspice, stir well and keep in a covered container in a cool, dark place for about six weeks. Pack it in lidded baskets or clear glass jars or bottles with ribbons tied around the neck.

Homemade Musical Instruments from Natural or Recycled Objects

Drums   Cover the tops of large tins, boxes or plastic containers with greaseproof or architect's paper and secure it with a rubber band or glue. For the sticks use dessert sized spoons and for a softer sound wind some rags round the bowl. If old saucepans are used then cotton reels with an old pencil stuck in the middle will make a stronger sound.

Shakers   Put various objects such as pebbles, grit, seeds, dried peas, lentils etc in tins or other containers and close them. Children can guess what is in each tin.

Tinkling Sounds   Spare a few foil bottle tops from the collection and string them together to make a rattle. A bunch of old keys makes a good rhythmic sound and an assortment of small bells tied with string to a coathanger can make a peal.

Cymbals   If you can borrow two saucepan lids from the kitchen they make good cymbals.

Castanets   Two spoons taped together and tapped on the palm of one's hand are the simplest form. For a pair, fold in half two pieces of card, 12cm by 6cm, and stick two bottle tops exactly opposite each other on both cards.

Xylophone   Have a series of jam jars or bottles of the same size and put a different amount of water in each, going in sequence from almost full to almost empty. Tap gently with a spoon or whisk. Observe the differences in tone when you alter the amount of water.

Trumpets   These can be made out of cones: a semi-circle of card rolled up and glued to form a cone, with a mouthpiece cut out at the pointed end.

Mouth Organ   Place a piece of tissue paper round a comb and blow.

New Colours for Old Clothes   Natural dyes can be made from many different plants and fruits such as spinach, dogwood, coffee, raspberries, blueberries, onion skins, beetroot, walnut outer skins, golden rod. Soak the plants overnight making sure that the water covers them. Then strain and simmer the wet garment in the coloured water until the colour is the right shade, bearing in mind that it will be lighter when dry. To make the dye fast it will be necessary to add a mordant to the simmering process. Rubber gloves and adult help over the heating are recommended. As handkerchiefs are back in use instead of tissues, they can be given a new lease of life, also T-shirts.

Weaving   Most children have attempted some kinds of simple weaving; here are a few nature-orientated ideas:

Weave a Bird Hide   This should be near the bird table so that you can have a much closer view of the birds. Stake some 6′ bamboo canes at 6″ intervals making a semi-circular shape. Thread old brushwood and dead branches with leaves still attached in and out of the canes to make a solid hide with slots left at eye level.

Weave a bird hide

Flower Loom   Draw a circle on a piece of wood and hammer in nails round it at regular intervals, with one nail in the middle. Start weaving with thick wool from the centre and thread it round each nail in turn. Go round the circle three times until the flower pattern is quite distinct.

Large Woven Flower   This is an outdoor version of the flower loom, done on a larger scale on the grass, with skewers or tent pegs to take the wool to make the outline. The circle can be filled in with strips of coloured material, leaving the tips free to give a beautiful big flower.

Homemade Presents

Papier Maché Bowls   Very attractive bowls can be made out of papier maché using an earthenware or china bowl as moulds either inside or outside, according to whether you want a foot. Then cut out coloured pictures of flower heads from magazines and seed catalogues and cover both sides of the bowl with them, sticking them with glue. The last layer of the papier maché could be real pressed leaf or flower petals, choosing the ones that have kept their colour.

Make a papier maché bowl. Decorate with flowers and leaves cut out from magazines etc. Stick on with glue

Grapefruit Skin Boxes Choose one half of a grapefruit that is slightly larger than the other and fit both halves on to the bottoms of plastic juice bottles, round or square and allow to dry for several days. Then see that the two halves fit and paint, decorate and varnish them.

Make Paper Flowers Cut out a number of circles of tissue paper and sew or wire them together in the middle. Braid a wire stem with green paper. Carnations can be made by gluing quarter circles to a whole circle; serrate the edges with scissors. They can be made of white, pink or red tissue paper.

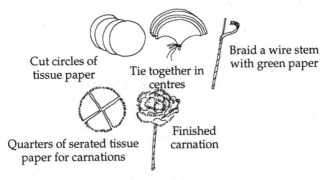

Cut circles of tissue paper

Tie together in centres

Braid a wire stem with green paper

Quarters of serated tissue paper for carnations

Finished carnation

Make paper flowers

Decorated Plastic Plant Pots You can paint designs on these pots or cover them with paper mosaic and then varnish them. Give them as presents complete with a plant that you have grown.

Painted Stones Choose interesting stones that you have collected and paint them with enamel paints. Large round ones can be used as paper weights and tiny flat ones as brooches with a brooch pin glued on to the back.

Raffia Bracelets Wind raffia or wool round a cardboard ring and embroider it with flower patterns.

Making Things to Play With

Animal in a Cage   Draw or paste a picture of a lion or tiger on a square card and then turn the card over and upside down to draw the cage. Punch a hole at opposite sides of the card halfway down. Thread a rubber band through each side and wind up by twisting the bands. When it is untwisted the illusion is of the lion or tiger in the cage.

Colour Spinner   Cut out a circle in thin card and divide it into four quarters and colour them on both sides in different colours. Bore two holes opposite each other near the centre and thread through a long piece of thin string and tie the ends together. Make loops at either side of the circle and put a finger in each and twist the string tightly. Then let it unspin and see what happens to the colours on either side.

Spinner Top   Colour the circle as described above on one side only. Insert a small sharp pencil through the middle and spin. Are the colours the same?

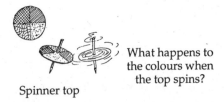

What happens to
the colours when
the top spins?

Spinner top

A Butterfly Life Cycle   Cut out two rounds of thin card and draw the four stages of the butterfly in each corner of one circle and then cut out windows to match the drawings in the other circle. Fasten them in the centre with a round paper clip and by turning the top circle you can illustrate the complete cycle through the windows. This can be done with other insects such as dragon flies, or with frogs.

Make a Fishpond Game   Paint a square cardboard box without a lid on the outside with a pond scene: water weeds and flowers, pond creatures, and different kinds of fish. Cut out cardboard fish about one or two inches long and fix a steel paper clip on each of them. Make fishing rods with sticks or canes with fine string and a small magnet tied to the end. Take it in turns to pick up a fish by magnetism.

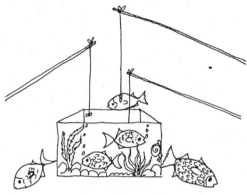

Make a fish pond

Homemade Skittles   Fasten papier maché heads on to the tops of plastic bottles and paint them. If necessary weigh them down with some sand so that they are stable.

Tin Stilts   Take two solid tins with lids attached and bore two holes in each one and thread string round each pair of holes, using enough to hold as two sets of reins. The holes may have to be bored by the adults and the size of tins should fit the feet.

Constructions

Landscapes   There are various materials to construct landscapes with, such as clay and plasticine. Homemade play dough is particularly suitable. The recipe is to mix together a cup of flour, half a cup of salt, two teaspoonfuls of Cream of Tartar and a cup of water and a tablespoon of oil. Then stir over medium heat until it has the consistency of bread dough and it can be kneaded in the same way. It will keep for a time in an air tight container. The children can use their imagination in constructing mountains, rivers, dams and reservoirs or models of a village, a farm or a castle.

Recipe for homemade playdough

Co-operative Collages Cut out shapes from wrapping paper, foil and luxurious fabrics and glue the designs on to card. This process lends itself to collaborative murals of scenes from nature: woodlands, parks, flower gardens or the seaside. It can be shared by all of the family or friends, each one making a contribution and sticking it on.

Mosaics Many different materials can be used for mosaics: pieces of shell, fabrics and foil to be stuck together to make miniature pictures of landscapes. One idea is to paint clean dry egg shells in bright colours, break them into pieces and stick on paper.

Chapter IV

Gardens for Children

A garden is a lovesome plot,
God wot.

So many families live in urban flats that this chapter might seem irrelevant for them. However there are many possibilities of growing plants outside the house, even if you haven't got a garden: just as we found how many miniature gardens could flourish indoors. It is exciting for children to have their own little 'plot'; and even if it is only a window box, a hanging basket or a tub on a narrow balcony, they can take pleasure in planning it themselves with a little help from the adults.

Other alternatives are allotments which several families could share or a part of a neighbour's garden, as people are often too busy to tend to them these days; also many elderly neighbours might welcome children who would plant a patch full of annuals, which always give a colourful display.

So let us first explore container gardening, both for those who have no more space and for those who want to enhance their backyards and gardens.

Hanging Baskets   These are so worthwhile, even if you have to get a long bracket fixed near your window to secure them, or alternatively to have them hanging on either side of the porch or front door. Older children can make their own baskets with a few thin wire coat hangers and a pair of pliers, making sure that the weave is close enough to hold the plants in position. Line the basket with fresh damp moss and peat substitute or a fibre lining, then make a base of small stones and some charcoal and fill in with good potting soil and compost, leaving a shallow hole in the middle to collect water. You can plant them with sweet smelling, colourful flowers like geraniums, fushias, marigolds and all sorts of herbs, with trailers like lobelia and ivies to fill up the sides. Soak the basket in water before hanging up and remember that all plants in containers need more water and food than the ones on the ground.

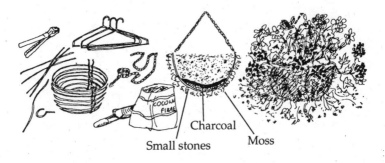

Charcoal

Small stones   Moss

Hanging baskets

Window Boxes   If you can saw three planks of wood and two squares for the ends and nail them together, this will be a good experience for the children to participate, otherwise there are plenty of choices of window boxes on the market. It is important to see that they are treated to withstand the weather and have drainage holes drilled at the base and wedges of wood for the box to stand on. Children can collect stones and pebbles for the bottom layer and add plenty of charcoal; and then when it is securely fixed on the window sill, build up layers of compost and potting soil. They can plant their window garden with the upright flowers like petunias, dahlias and mignonelle at the back and hanging plants like fuschias, nasturtiums, geraniums and variegated ivy to hide the box. Planting can be done with spoons and forks wired to long sticks and children should be supervised in case they lean out too far!

Window boxes

Balcony Containers and Tubs These need the same care as window boxes, but have greater potential for variety: shrubs like buddleias are very easy to grow from cuttings; rose and even apple trees can be successful in large tubs. They can be protected from drying out by having a layer of mulch on the surface such as decayed leaves or bark chips. All sorts of vegetables and salads can flourish in gro-bags, especially tomatoes; and a favourite with the children will be a strawberry pot. They will be able to take care of the watering until the great day when they can pick and eat their produce. Make sure that a perforated tube is inserted down the middle of the strawberry pot to distribute the water evenly.

Herbs

Plant a Herb Garden Most herbs like the sun and do not want too much water. You can grow oregano, basil, sage, mint, lemon balm, chives and parsley from seed. Parsley seeds should be soaked in warm water the day before planting and even then they take a long time to appear, although they can then last for two years and often self-seed after that. A bunch of mint in a jar of water can root within a week if it is kept in a sunny position; it can then be planted in a pot or contained in a tin with the top and bottom removed, as it can spread too rapidly.

New Herbs from Old   You can take cuttings from sage in
spring or summer, whereas rosemary gets new plants from
cuttings taken only in late summer. Rosemary branches can also
be pinned down to the earth and will produce new roots. You
can divide chives and plant in pots and if you keep cutting they
will keep growing. With thyme you divide a small piece
together with some roots in the spring.

Drying Herbs   Harvest them on a sunny day and hang them
to dry in a cool place. When the herbs are quite dry the children
can rub them through their fingers and store them in recycled
jars. Thyme, marjoram, sage, mint and lemon balm all dry well.

Herbs can appeal to children for many reasons: they can grow
them easily in their window boxes and containers to attract the
butterflies and bees and also to keep away enemy insects. When
dried they can use them in simple recipes and make scented
pillows and bags and concoct perfumes and shampoos with the
sweet smelling ones.

Drying herbs

A Bath for Tired Feet   Steep some rosemary and mint in hot
water and when it has cooled sufficiently, soak your tired feet
in it.

Frozen Herb Cubes   Put a teaspoonful of dried herbs into
each cube and fill with water and use for soups when required.

Frozen herb cubes

Herb Recipes   You can sprinkle fresh or dried herbs on your salads, soups, quiches and pizzas. You can make a herb pot-pourri, blending them with scented flower petals.

Herb Shampoos   Mix four parts of pure liquid soap with one part of olive oil and add two teaspoonfuls of chopped herbs: rosemary, thyme, lemon balm, and pour into a container with a lid and store it in a cool place. In a couple of weeks it can be strained and used as a shampoo or a body cleanser.

Herb Pillows and Bags   These can be made simply by sewing three sides of double fabric on the wrong side. Turn inside out and stuff with sweet smelling dried herbs and oversew the last side. These can be used to induce sleep, and to perfume the bath, to freshen clothes and to keep away moths, which do not like the smell of lavender and mint with a dash of cinnamon added. A herb sachet placed in your pet's basket will help to repel the fleas. A headache cushion made of peppermint and spearmint with a little eau de cologne mint can work miracles.

Herb Perfumes   Fill a pint jug with herbs; lemon balm and thyme make a good combination, and pour on hot water. Leave for a few hours, then pour into fancy decorated bottles.

Herb pillows and bags

Lavender Bundles   Dry a bunch of lavender stalks in the sun and tie a long coloured ribbon just under the heads. Gently bend the stalks back over the heads and secure the ends with an elastic band. Thread the two ribbons in and out so that the bundle of heads looks like a basket. Tie the ribbons in a bow at the end of the bundle.

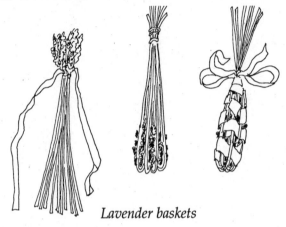

Lavender baskets

Herbal Teas   Camomile is soothing for toothache; fennel and mint for digestion, and sage for a gargle for sore throats.

A Garden of Your Own   If children are fortunate enough to have a real garden, however small, this can be a great delight. Annuals are easy to grow and they can produce a riot of colour. Canterbury bells, cornflowers, clarkias, candytuft, nemesias, french marigolds and sweetpeas are all old favourites and can be grown from seed. Deadheading can be satisfying for children and flowers like pansies, sweetpeas and roses will keep on producing more and more flowers if there are none that are going to seed.

Making a Wildlife Garden   A mini-wildlife garden can attract plenty of insects: nettles, which are beloved of the peacock butterfly and the red admiral are best contained in order to prevent spreading. The Buddleia, which is well named the butterfly tree, grows really quickly in pots and the sweet smelling tobacco plant attracts moths in the early evening with its perfume.

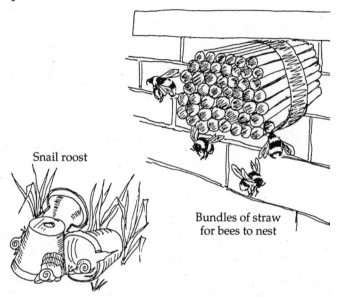

Snail roost

Bundles of straw for bees to nest

Making a wildlife garden

If you have room to plant larger bushes, the hawthorn attracts many insects with its heavily scented blossom and it is popular with the birds because of its red haws. So are the cotoneasters, firethorns and of course the holly. A corner of the garden left to grow grass like a meadow does not need a lot of space and wild seeds such as moon daisies can be nurtured. As almost all of our meadow land has been ploughed up to make room for vast areas of arable land, your tiny 'meadow' is a small contribution to help restore it.

A rockery with unusually shaped rocks and some decaying logs will attract many of the 'creepy crawlies' like woodlice. Grow bee borage to entice the bees, and a bundle of brightly coloured drinking straws will invite small bees to make a nest inside them. A snail roost can be made by leaving broken pots in damp areas and the snails can be marked underneath on their shells to see if the same ones come back. Of course if they are eating your dahlias or lettuces, they might well be taken for a ride when caught.

Try growing cow parsley as a home for ladybirds and if you have the space a giant hog weed is a special favourite of theirs and is beginning to be rare and therefore protected.

Attracting Wild Mammals to your Garden

Dormice   just might take up the offer of old tennis balls as a home in a secluded spot in the thickest part of a hedge; there would have to be an entrance hold and the balls securely nailed to a post. As so many of our hedges have been destroyed, dormice are getting scarce, so they need all the hospitality they can get.

Hedgehogs   It would be exciting to have a hedgehog living in your garden, so a wooden or strong cardboard box, camouflaged with leaves and filled with straw and with a short length of pipe for an entrance might do the trick. It would appreciate a saucer of bread and milk served up in the evening.

Attracting animals to your garden
(hedgehog)

Bats   are real friends of the earth and it is a shame that they have such an undeserved reputation of blood sucking and getting caught in women's hair. As they can eat as many as 3,500 insects in one night, most of them being of the unfriendly sort, it is worth making a bat box to entice them. It can be constructed out of rough wood with an entrance of about 18mm on the underside through which they can crawl. It should be mounted high up in a tree, facing south to keep the young bats warm.

Make a Mini-pond   You can make a pond as small as 40" by 20", either dug out in the garden or in a large container or old sink. If it is in the garden, you dig a hole about 8" deep and completely line it with a thick layer of old newspaper or a piece

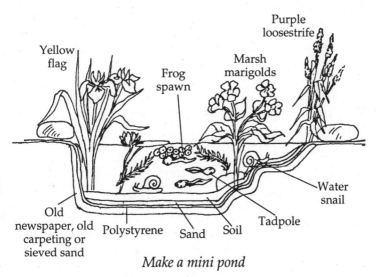

Purple loosestrife

Yellow flag

Frog spawn

Marsh marigolds

Water snail

Old newspaper, old carpeting or sieved sand   Polystyrene   Sand   Soil   Tadpole

Make a mini pond

of old carpeting or sieved sand. Then spread a sheet of polythene over it, or an old carpet large enough to overlap round the edges which should be secured with large stones. Put a layer of sand at the bottom and then a layer of soil and fill the mini-pond with pond water. Baby irises can be planted round the sides, also marsh marigolds, purple loosestrife and water forget-me-nots and in the water itself, water plantain or water stalwort. Avoid duckweed as it spreads so rapidly over a pond. As the pond is so small you would have to choose one or two species only, but if there is room around the pond, primulas and violets will like the damp atmosphere. There will not be much space for many pond creatures, but water snails will keep the pond fresh and frog and toad spawn can be introduced in the spring, as long as there is access to rocks once they develop legs. If you have been pond dipping, you could bring home some caddis lavae and sticklebacks, but avoid dragon fly nymphs and the great diving beetle, as they will eat any other pond creatures.

Seeds

It is truly wondrous that contained in a tiny seed are the means to produce a perfect plant and even a gigantic tree. This is of course with the help of the sun and with nourishment from the ground and the air.

Gather Your Own Seeds   Wait until the seeds are really ripe and make sure that they are dry before putting them into envelopes to store in a cool dry place during the winter months. Seeds from pods like wallflowers, lupins, honesty and any of the pea and bean family are easy to manage.

Sunflower Seeds   Surely the most satisfying seeds to grow are the sunflowers. You can almost watch them grow taller and turn their heads towards the sun. When the flower is over and the seeds begin to ripen, cut off the stalk about ten inches from the head and hang it in a dry place. When the seeds are quite dry rub them off the head and store them in a tin.

Toasted Sunflower Seeds   Put them in a frying pan or in a moderate oven with a teaspoonful of salt and grill or bake them for five minutes, shaking the pan or stirring the oven ones halfway through.

Toasted sunflower seeds

Sunflower Chocolate Balls Mix together equal quantities of sunflower seeds, honey and grated chocolate and roll the balls in sesame seeds. This is a very nutritious delicacy as well as being quite delicious.

Pumpkin Seeds Follow the recipes for sunflower seeds and also grind a mixture of pumpkin, sunflower and sesame seeds, which are great to sprinkle on soups or salads. Parents sometimes use the seeds in helping their children to count, filling plastic cups with tens and bigger ones with hundreds.

Everlasting Flowers from Seed There is an everlasting sweetpea which is easy to grow and often will self-seed and come up year after year. Dry the seeds in the normal way and plant in early spring. Bunches of the flowers can by hung to dry in a cool room and the everlasting species are more likely to keep their appearance as an indoor display.

Rather than plant seeds straight into the garden, they can be started indoors or in a mini-greenhouse or cold frame. This will help the seedlings to get strong before being planted out.

Making a Mini-Greenhouse Plastic containers or even jam jars can be used as miniature greenhouses, but if you want something bigger to warm up the seedlings you can make a frame of bamboo and cover it with thin plastic, leaving the base open so that it can be moved to operate as a large cloche where it is needed.

Plastic container

Bamboo and plastic cloche

Jam jars

Making a mini greenhouse

Making a Cold Frame Line a wooden slatted orange box with clear plastic. Cover with heavy clear plastic weighed down at each long end.

Summer Salads   You can make gro-bags with your own rich compost contained in black bags. Sow lettuce weekly from early spring and you will be able to cut them in early morning in the summer. Young radishes straight from the garden are delicious and children can cut them into decorative flowers. Cover the seeds of cucumber with a jam jar placed on a ridge of earth or a gro-bag, and when seven leaves have formed pinch the top ones back to make the side shoots grow. Dwarf bushes of tomatoes can be grown anywhere that is sunny and sheltered and children can have their own pot of cherry tomatoes.

One Potato, Two Potatoes   Plant a potato by clearing a small patch of ground and putting one or two potatoes on top of the soil, covering them with thick black polythene with little holes where the sprouts will come through. Put stones down to keep the polythene in place and water when needed. I used to love digging up new potatoes, cooking them and then eating them with chopped mint; there is something very special about planting and then digging up that will appeal to all ages.

Runner Bean Wigwams   Plant the beans in late spring when it is warm and make a wigwam of long stakes with one bean to each stick which they can twine around. When they begin to flower spray them with water to help set the flowers and, like the deadheading process, keep picking the young pods so that the plant keeps on producing.

Runner bean wigwams

Flowers from Vegetables   We often forget that vegetables can have very attractive flowers such as the round purple heads of the onion family. Just let some of them keep growing until they flower.

Children will be enthusiastic about growing unusual plants, such as pumpkins for Halloween, gourds for decoration, loofahs for the bathroom and Japanese-type bonsai trees.

Grow a Pumpkin   Plant the seeds one inch deep on a patch of rich soil or in a container, after they have been soaked overnight. If they are planted in the summer, they should be ready by Halloween as long as they are given lots of water. To grow a really big one for a mask, pinch off the little flower heads at the ends of the vines.

Make a Pumpkin Mask   Cut off the top and scoop out the flesh; then cut out eyes, nose and mouth and put a night light candle inside to make a lantern. Use the flesh to make a pumpkin pie. Besides being tasty to eat, pumpkin seeds can be made into necklaces or collage patterns by sticking them on card.

Make a pumpkin mask and seed necklace

Gourds for Decoration   Plant gourds from a packet of mixed cucurbita seeds in a sunny spot, water regularly and place sticks for them to climb up. Pick the gourds on a warm day when the fruits have become quite dry. Leave them to dry out for a few days, clean and polish them and then coat them with clear varnish to keep their colour. They can be given as presents and used as table decorations.

Loofahs to Scrub Your Backs   Grow the loofah seeds as for the gourds and pick them at the end of the growing season, putting them in a warm place to dry out. When they are quite dry, peel off their skins to make loofahs.

How to Make a Bonsai Tree   These are miniature trees, which the Japanese are expert in shaping. The secret is to take a seedling and cut back its roots and branches continually and the tree will gradually become dwarfed.

Carve Your Name   When cucumbers, marrows, pumpkins or gourds are big enough to carve a child's name on the skin, it will become enlarged as they grow. This is a favourite game with flower seeds which can be sown in the form of a name or even a slogan! Small annuals like virginia stock are specially suitable for this treatment.

Carve your name

Organic Gardening   The great thing about organic gardening is that it relies on natural processes to build and rebuild the soil, instead of using chemical fertilisers and pesticides, which are dangerous to all living plants and creatures, including our children. Besides polluting the soil they seep through the earth and contaminate the waterways and eventually the ocean. The basis of the organic garden is that it is nourished with homemade compost.

Making Compost   If you put every bit of vegetable waste into a special bin, you will have plenty of material to make good compost: fruit peelings and skins, vegetable scraps, tea leaves and bags, coffee grounds, eggshells etc. Layer garden soil alternately with six inches of refuse and the same amount of plant and grass cuttings or torn up newspaper, aerating it with additions of twigs and large weeds and watering each layer as you build it up. Compost can be stored in a hole in the ground about one metre square or in a container made of chicken wire, as illustrated. If you have very little space, you can make compost in a bucket, which should be pierced on all sides to let the air in and never allowed to dry out. The compost should be stirred every few weeks and after some months it will supply nourishing food for your garden and indoor plants.

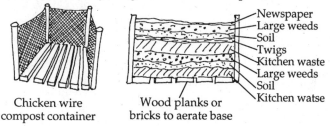

Chicken wire
compost container

Wood planks or
bricks to aerate base

Newspaper
Large weeds
Soil
Twigs
Kitchen waste
Large weeds
Soil
Kitchen watse

Section through compost

Making compost

An Organic Fertiliser   You can make your own by picking nettles, (using strong gloves), and packing them into a bucket. Fill it with water and cover it for two weeks and use the strained liquid on your plants.

Encouraging Friendly Insects Organic gardening is concerned with the encouragement of predators that will feed on creatures that destroy our crops. It is good for children to know more about 'creepy crawlies', which they often regard with revulsion. By taking an active interest in them, the children

'Creepy crawly' habitat

can overcome these feelings and realise the part they play in the whole scheme of things. Ladybirds have always been popular with children and would still be so even if they didn't eat hundreds of aphids that attack our roses and dahlias amongst many other plants. Centipedes might not have the same charm as ladybirds, but they consume lots of unfriendly insect larvae as do the ground beetles. Frogs and toads do splendid work in demolishing caterpillars, woodlice, slugs and all sorts of enemy insects.

To attract friendly insects you can make a mixture of one part honey, one part yeast and three parts water and put it under the vulnerable plants. This will attract nectar seeking insects which will pollinate your flowers.

Ladybird   Ground   Froglet
                beetle   a good
                              predator in
                              garden

Encouraging friendly insects

Trapping Enemy Insects   It might be difficult for children to distinguish between friendly centipedes and enemy milli-pedes: millipedes have two legs to each segment and not of course, one thousand in all, and they just love the insides of roots of vegetables and bulbs. They can be trapped in hollowed-out turnips or parsnips; and in the same way, woodlice can be caught in hollowed-out apples. Slugs will be attracted to a scooped-out half orange or grapefruit, placed like an igloo with a door cut for an entrance. Slugs and snails can easily be caught after rain in the evening; and a really exciting adventure for the children is to search for them after dark with a torch covered with red paper, so that the creatures are not scared away by the light. They could keep them in a vivarium until the next day, when they could take them to some waste land to begin a new life! I find the idea of a 'beer trap' too heartless, although beer drinkers might feel that this is a good way to go!

The Gardener's Best Friend   This is certainly the earthworm. If you are sitting on the ground there would probably be over a dozen just underneath you! The aerate the ground with their maze of tunnels and they eat all sorts of plant matter, which they drag down from the surface, so they are the real diggers. They can even tell you what kind of soil they are in: if it is water-logged or poor, the worm is likely to be pale, but if it is well drained and rich, the worm will be a dark red colour.

Companion Planting   This method is part of wise folklore, long before we heaped poison onto our soil: the idea is to include the right companions to grow together such as onions in between rows of all kinds of the cabbage family, or strong herbs amongst the tomatoes. In fact all herbs help to confuse the insect pests which rely mainly on their sense of smell to get to the plant they desire.

Non-toxic Spraying   Children can mix up a solution of water and pure soap, which they can flake from left-over ends. Alternatively they can make a concoction of water that has stood for 24 hours soaked in chopped onions or garlic and strained. They will probably prefer the soap recipe! These solutions can be sprayed frequently on to any plants that are attacked by insect pests.

For those who want something stronger without resorting to toxic pesticides, I have been given a recipe which can be used for sprays against blackfly, whitefly and greenfly, snails, cabbage flies, mosquitos and some caterpillars. Apparently these creatures, like some humans, cannot tolerate the smell of garlic! You pulverise three large garlic cloves and add 6 table-spoons of paraffin and leave in a bowl for 48 hours. Then grate 1 table-spoon of soap into a pint of hot water and stir, and when it is melted mix with the garlic pulp and strain. Use 2 table-spoons of mixture to 4 pints of water and spray with a 'natural pesticide' re-usable spray.

Birds in the Garden

The most fascinating of all the creatures that visit the garden are surely the birds. Children who have no outdoor space can still attract them by having bird trays hinged to the window sills or even using the sills, as long as they are wide enough. They can construct window hides with brown paper and a slit for viewing the antics of the tits and the swarms of sparrows and starlings.

Even if you have the smallest of gardens there could be room for a bird table and perhaps a bird bath and the fun that the children get from watching and listening to them will repay any loss of space.

Making a Bird Table   The simplest kind of bird table takes the form of a square tray with slots of wood around it to prevent the food from falling off, leaving spaces at the corners for cleaning. It should be nailed to a post which can stand in the earth or be fixed to a solid wooden base. This easy carpentry will be within the capabilities of many children, with some guidance from the adults. Old trays can be re-used for this purpose, attached to branches of a tree or the window sill, with string threaded through the holes made at each corner. In placing your table make sure that the birds will be able to spot any prowling cats well in advance.

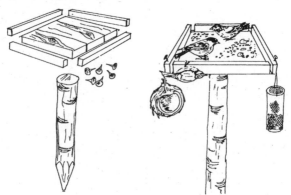

Making a bird table

Feeding the Birds   If we start feeding the birds during the winter months we should continue until we wean them in the early spring when nesting begins, as then the parent birds need to forage for suitable food for their young. Children will love making special concoctions for their birds: some ideas might be to hang up empty fir cones spread with dripping or peanut butter; these are as popular with tits as are half coconuts.

Even the half coconuts can be recycled by filling them with bird cake mixture: crumbled up bread, pastry, cooked rice, porridge, bacon rind chopped finely, grated cheese, dried fruit, apples cut in quarters, all bound together with fat! An original idea for recycling old scrubbing brushes could be to cover them with fat and then roll in seeds and hang up; if there are no brushes around, then a log with holes drilled in would serve the same purpose. A necklace of dried fruit and peanuts can be easily threaded with fine string, and if the children grow sunflowers, they can hang the dried heads upside down as a special feast. They can also collect bunches of weeds such as groundsel and docks when they are in seed and hang them in the garden. A good way to protect any of the hanging feeders from the rain is to make a hole in a plastic plate and thread the string through it so that it faces downwards. This makes it more difficult for squirrels to eat up all the goodies.

Dealing with Bully Birds   How often one sees the smaller birds being frightened away by the larger ones, like pigeons, magpies or jays. One solution is to make domes of chicken wire, securing the edges with stones. After a time the small ones will pluck up courage to get through the holes whereas the bigger ones are left outside.

A Permanent Water Trough for the Birds   Birds need water just as much as food, especially in winter when you might have to break the ice. Better still you can make a permanent water supply by fixing two pieces of wood together to make an L-shaped stand and wiring it to a post or tree trunk. Bore two holes just below the neck of a large plastic bottle, fill it with water and with the cap firmly screwed on, reverse it over a plastic saucer, resting on the L-shaped support. The bottle can now be wired to the support and the water will gradually trickle down to replenish the saucer.

A permanent water trough for birds

Bird Baths   As birds love to play in water a bird bath will attract them: this can be an old dustbin lid with the handle taken off, or a basin or a bucket with a dead shrub for them to perch in. When I tried to revive a wilted azalea in a bucket of water I found a host of sparrows on its branches and taking dives to splash in the water!

Bird bath

Breaking the Ice   In very cold weather a night light under a metal container of water will be very welcome, or, if you have a pond, float a rubber ball on it when it is likely to freeze over. This will also provide oxygen for the pond creatures.

A Dust Bath for Birds   As dustbins usually wear out before their lids, you might have another lid to spare. Use it as for the water bath and fill it with dust or very fine sand and the birds will roll in it to clean their feathers. If there is a danger of cats pouncing on them, it is best to screw the lids to a square post wedged in the earth or on a criss-cross stand. (When we are even recycling our dust we can claim to be really ecologically minded!)

Birds and Their Nests

Making Nest Boxes   With old trees being felled or blown down in the storms and 95% of the hedgerows having been destroyed, there is a real shortage of places where birds can nest, so see if you can entice them into your homemade nest box, as illustrated. This will be quite a challenge for young carpenters, but they will be proud of sawing according to the measurements and then screwing the parts together, making sure to bore holes at the bottom for drainage and at the back to fix it on a tree. The most difficult job is to drill out the entrance hole; you will have to decide which birds you aim to attract and make the hole to fit them: 27mm in diameter for coal tits and 30mm for great tits, which are the most likely to take advantage of your hospitality, especially if you have put some dried grass inside. Further details for bird box building can be obtained from the RSPB 'Action for Birds' campaign, which also gives information on making bat boxes.

The boxes should be installed by February and then a very quiet watch should be kept to see if any birds are using it; it may take a time before it is occupied, but it is well worth the wait.

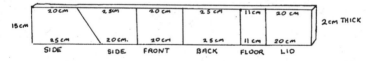

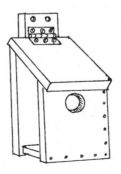

Making nest boxes

Providing Nest Materials   You will be doing a good turn to the birds if you provide nest materials which are in short supply. Hang some of the combings from your hair on bushes, other ingredients could be any kind of stuffing, cotton wool, strands of wool, hay, animal hair, fine twigs, down feathers and even some wet mud. If you find an old abandoned nest (birds make new ones for the next year), this will give you ideas as to what that particular bird might require. The children could try to make their own birds nests and they will realise how clever the birds are to make them so intricately.

Berries for Birds   If you have enough space, plant shrubs specially for the birds: holly, cotoneaster and hawthorn are easy to grow and will provide beautiful berries in the winter when food is scarce.

Frightening the Birds Away   Make a mobile of chimes that will tinkle in the wind: if you cut out shapes from aluminium containers, they will flash in the sunlight scaring the birds. Beautiful chimes can also be made from a variety of sea shells strung together with string.

Frightening the birds away

Scarecrows   The children can have fun creating a scarecrow out of straw or brushwood and old clothes. Why not a woman scarecrow? They do as much gardening as men! Of course your aim may be to attract the birds rather than scare them away. In that case would they venture to take delicacies from your scarecrow such as coconut halves, cones with fat and nuts, and peanut necklaces? You may consider that it is worthwhile having the birds as neighbours and observing them, even if they do eat some of the seeds you plant; after all they will eat many of your unfriendly insect pests as well!

Scarecrows (woman)

Bird Song

Spot the Song   Children need help in identifying bird songs and unless you have a knowledgeable adult to accompany them, it is best to rely upon cassettes. These can be obtained from the RSPB and their ones specially recommended for beginners are: 'British Wildlife Habitats No 5', 'The Garden' and 'Bird Spot'. 'More British Wild Birds in Stereo' and 'Woodland and Garden Birds' are from BBC Records. After listening, children can see if they can identify the songs. They could take the cassette where the habitat of the particular bird is and see if they can get a response.

Tape Your Own Bird Song   Fix a cone of thin card on to the microphone of your tape recorder and try to capture some well known bird songs. I have a resident song thrush that sings in a tree near my window every evening as it is getting dusk, he seems to be the only bird singing at that time. You could manage to entice a robin with the tape recording and get its belligerent call as he thinks another robin is on his territory. Wood pigeons are easy to distinguish, as are peewits; and blackbirds can be identified as they fly in low swoops to trees in the garden. If you ever have the chance to hear a nightingale, it is worthwhile being woken up and a tape recording would be crystal clear at that time of night. Use your cassette as a quiz game to see how many bird songs your friends can spot.

Tape your own bird song

Bird Calls Play the cassettes, one bird song at a time, and get everyone to write down their idea of what it is saying; there is no right or wrong in this imaginative activity and each one will probably have a different version, except the cuckoo's call! The peewit or plover seems to trail over the word, 'Peeeee wit' and we always said that the yellow hammer calls out 'A little piece of bread and no-o cheese'!

Communicating with Birds I once imitated a melodious bird song as I was going to a meeting in the heart of the country. To my surprise I received an answer back and we then continued back-wards and forwards, until to my shame I had to go, and I felt I had really let my 'partner' down!

Chapter V

Exploring the Elements

All children have an innate fascination for the elements; earth, air, fire and water; and it is their rightful heritage to be able to face and explore them.

Earth Encounters   The qualities of earth can be explored through sand play, growing plants and modelling clay. In the old days in the country, children would make mud pies and cakes with elderberries and hips and haws as fruit; and there is still a lot to be said for playing and painting with mud! To be able to mould clay or sand in any way the children please is a creative and empowering exercise and highly therapeutic.

Decorated mud pie

Clay Diggers   If you have access to clay in your garden or in the field of a friendly farmer, it is much more satisfying to dig it up yourself. It will need quite a lot of 'knocking up', kneading and slapping into shape, and the foreign bodies removed. Then models can be made of creatures and landscapes and, if you can get it fired, then hollow out all the thick parts, otherwise it will explode in the kiln! (See Chapter 3 on Making Things.)

Bas Relief Sculptured reliefs can be carved out of slabs of clay, depicting scenes of animals in their habitats, or landscapes with reliefs of hills, valleys and rivers, and hung up like pictures on the wall.

Dig for Treasure Aspiring archaeologists should always wear strong gloves and leave the site exactly as they found it. All kinds of soil can be concealing some of earth's treasures; you might even find some Roman remains! Coins and pieces of old pottery can sometimes be found and often some surprises. Ceramic pieces can be made into mosaics, implanted in clay or plaster of Paris. In reality, you are much more likely to find some indestructible plastic, which shows the true nature of non-biodegradable material. Your own garden can reveal some barely remembered items, like a lost toy, but of course if you dig elsewhere you must get permission. When you have made quite a collection, you can wash the treasures and display your finds in a joint effort, and this might inspire a later interest in archaeology.

Dig for treasure

Digging Up the Pots First make your pots out of clay and decorate them with paint and, if possible, make them look antique. Then, if you can bear it, break them up into large pieces and bury them. Have a dig and unearth the pieces and stick them together, just as a professional archaeologist would do.

Biodegradable Experiment   Choose a selection of items that get put in the dustbin, such as paper, pieces of fabric, cardboard, sweet wrappers, an aluminium and a steel tin, a polystyrene container, a plastic cup, a nail, etc and bury them in the earth. Look to see what has happened after a month, after two months.

Fossils   Look for fossils in areas of limestone and try to find ammonites; these are coiled creatures turned into stone over millions of years. There are amazing examples of all kinds of fossils in the geological museums.

Crystals   There are many crystals that you can make by dissolving minerals to saturation point, but the favourite is undoubtedly candied sugar. To crystallise it round a string, you heat half a cup of water and gradually add a whole cup of sugar, stirring until it has all been dissolved. Then pour the solution into a glass jar which has a weighted string hanging down the middle, strung to a pencil balanced over the top. The candied sugar will take a week or two to form round the string, and all you have to do is to see that no crust forms on top of the syrup by occasionally stirring it. When we made it as children, it was the best sweet that we ever tasted!

Making Bricks   Choose a plastic container the size of an average brick and coat the inside with vaseline or line it with cling film and fill it with damp clay, smoothing the top. When dry, the brick can be turned out to make room for the next one; better still, use several moulds of different sizes and then build a wall or a house, bearing in mind that as the bricks are not fired they will not withstand the rain. Alternatively, make a mould by pushing a brick into damp sand. When the brick is removed, fill the mould with plaster of Paris.

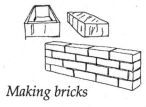

Making bricks

Stone Age Tools   If you have access to flints, try making tools as Stone Age people did. You will need protective goggles and then strike one flint against the other, which you can shape to be spearheads or various forms of cutters.

Rockwatch   This is a club run by "Watch" (the environmental club for young people) for young fans of fossils, rocks and dinosaurs. It runs competitions for collectors of rocks, such as limestone, slate, granite, chalk, flint, etc. which could entail submitting drawings and photographs, as well as actual collections. It also issues three magazines a year, giving information about dinosaurs, volcanoes and fossil finding, and suggests activities such as model building of layers of rock formation.

Useful Rocks   Look out for rocks that have special qualities such as smoothness, oval shape, different layers or lines. If there are unlimited quantities around, you could choose a very special one to be a paperweight, or a doorstop, or simply to hold and keep in your room.

Pebble Maps   Choose different shapes and colours of small pebbles and make a map or picture in mosaic form in a shallow garden saucer and glue down if it is to be permanent.

Visit a Geological Museum   Some adults might wonder if geological museums might be dull or too academic for children, but in fact they are fascinated by their wonderful range of rocks, crystals and minerals. They can handle all sorts of specimens and buy examples to start a collection.

Sand   Sand trays are ideal for imaginative play, not only with containers for pouring, emptying, moulding or modelling. Tiny

Sand (trays)

models of people, houses, trees and farms stand up beautifully in sand and can be moved around according to the fantasy. If possible, two trays are best; one with fine, dry sand and the other with wet sand.

Sand Out of Doors   There are many sources of sand to play with. Children can construct dams, dykes and bridges on the seashore and stream banks and on commons and heaths. Unless you are sure that the sea will wash smooth your constructions, always leave everything as you have found it, especially when building dams to divert a small stream. These activities might need permission and also some supervision from adults for safety reasons.

Sand Painting   Sprinkle different coloured sand over paper thinly spread with glue or paste. The most natural paintings are with different kinds of sand that you can grate into powder from soft rocks, otherwise you can colour it with powder paints.

Preserving Flowers and Plants in Sand   If the flowers are bulky like roses, they can be immersed in a box of fine, dry sand for several weeks and then used as decorations.

Sand Bottles   These have become a tourist attraction where there are different kinds of rocks in the vicinity. The idea is to fill a bottle with different layers of sand of various shades. Tilt the bottle as you fill it to make the divisions more interesting.

Sand bottles

Models out of Sand   These are fashioned out of damp sand that is not too wet. There has to be a firm base such as an animal sitting down or a creature naturally earth bound like a snail; whales and dolphins could be attempted on the grand scale at the seaside to draw attention to the danger to their species!

Models out of sand

Sand Sculptures   These are more permanent versions of the models out of sand. Make models of animals in the same way and then pour plaster of Paris over them, making sure that it penetrates into the nooks and crannies. When the plaster is dry, turn the model upside down and empty out the sand from the inside. The outside will have an attractive texture of plaster with traces of sand, or the plaster can have been sprinkled all over with different coloured sand before it was dry.

Having Fun With Air

The Invisible Element   Young children think that because they cannot see air, there is nothing there, but they can be shown that when they immerse an empty bottle under a bowl of water, the air escapes in bubbles.

Breathing Air   Breathing exercises help to make children (and adults) relaxed, and can be the basis of meditation, where they are only aware of their breath and this can create a feeling of stillness. Quite young children can appreciate this kind of relaxation for a short time and find that their powers of creativity are really awakened after meditation. For example, they have been known to paint wonderfully imaginative pictures after a quiet period of attending to their breathing or after a guided fantasy recounted by an adult.

Feeling Air   When children stretch their hands wide apart and then bring them together, they can feel the air that they displace and much more so if they do it quickly.

How Much Air Can You Breathe Out?   Fill a clear plastic jar with water and put it upside down in a container of water. Insert a length of plastic tubing in the top of the bottle, which will be placed on the bottom of the container as shown in the illustration. Blow into the other end of the plastic tube and see how much water you can displace.

How much air can you breathe out?

Fun With Balloons   Children love balloons and they are the mainstay of most children's parties. Blowing them up and letting them go with a rude noise as the air escapes is always a source of delight. They could have a balloon patting race to see which player patting a balloon goes the furthest without dropping it. To appreciate the magic of balloons they could watch the French film 'The Red Balloon'. But it is important not to let the helium balloons out of your hands as happens in the film, because when they soar up into the sky, they have to come down eventually and the chances are that they will land in the sea and be swallowed by fish, mistaking them for tasty anemones!

Clay Pipe Bubbles   We all know the bubble blowing sets that we can buy, but the children could make clay pipes out of quick-drying clay and experiment with them in blowing bubbles with soap. This was a favourite pastime when many men smoked with clay pipes and the children would be given a new one to play with. They could also experiment with wire twisting to make different sizes of circles to blow bigger and bigger bubbles.

Clay pipe bubbles

Blowing Games   Make blowpipes with hollow bamboo, dried elder branches or straws and think how many blowing games you can invent: for example, a feather or balloon race (the balloon could be blown by or attached to the pipe by the suction of the breath), blowing peas into a hole, blow football with a ping-pong ball and two goal posts made out of coathangers and netting, with teams of two or three competing by blowing the ball with their pipes.

Air Pollution   It has always been said that the one thing in the world that is completely free is the air that we breathe. It may be free, but it is becoming increasingly polluted by the various gases released by our industrial societies causing smog or low level ozone damage, acid rain, the greenhouse effect and

Air pollution detectives (leaf test)

the destruction of the ozone layer, as well as widespread respiratory health problems. Children are becoming aware of these dangers and are often eager to take part in experiments to reveal the extent of the pollution of the air. They like to be treated as responsible people who can find out for themselves what the dangers are.

Air Pollution Detectives

Spot the Effects of Acid Rain   As you go for a walk, see if you can identify any obvious effects of acid rain: for example, conifers losing too many of their needles, deciduous trees shedding their leaves early and growing less foliage; the stone of ancient buildings being eaten away in their extremities, such as gargoyles and turrets.

Leaf Test   Collect all sorts of leaves from various places in the garden, the town centre, the roadside, the motorway and woodland areas, etc. and wipe them with cotton wool, or wash them with detergent and filter the water. Which places produce the dirtiest leaves? They could write to the local paper about their findings; children are more likely to get a hearing than adults.

Leaving your Cards   You can perform a similar experiment to the leaf test, using squares of card or plastic, or blank slides to examine the dirt through a microscope smeared with a thick layer of vaseline on the exposed side. The cards can be placed in more built-up areas than in the leaf test where there are fewer leaves to collect, and you can compare the results.

A Lichen Hunt   If you find leafy or bushy lichens, it shows that the air is relatively clean, but crusty lichens mean that the air is quite dirty and if there are no lichens at all where you might expect to find them, then the air is so dirty that none can grow. See if your findings coincide with the leaf test. Many large cities are completely devoid of lichens on their trees nowadays.

Smog Patrol   Take coat hangers and twist them into rectangles and stretch four rubber bands on each of them. Hang in various places where there might be polluted air and leave them for several weeks. If the air is heavily polluted, the rubber will have deteriorated and even broken; you can view them through a magnifying glass to see what changes have taken place. Rubber bands are found as litter on many city streets, having been thrown away by postmen as they undo their bundles of letters. It is interesting to note that rubber cultivation originated in the rain forests, as did so many products that we use and that synthetic rubber consumes more energy in its manufacture than natural rubber.

Smog patrol

Gathering Moss   Various metals, including poisonous lead, get trapped in moss, so you can collect small quantities of moss and send them to the local health authority to be analysed. The results might be an incentive to do things to make the air cleaner.

Tobacco Plant Test   Children can get two kinds of tobacco plant seeds from "Watch" which conducted a survey with children from all over the country on smog or low level ozone conditions. One species, Nicotiana Tabacum, produces black spots on leaves if it is contaminated with smog and the other is immune, which makes a reliable control.

Car Exhaust Tests   Take an odd white sock (many families have them!) or filter paper and get an adult to put it over the exhaust for a few minutes when the car is started. The results can be a message to install a CAT (catalytic converter) which changes the harmful gases into much less harmful ones. It only works with unleaded petrol, which more and more people are turning to, if their cars can use it.

Stop Smoking   Ask people not to smoke when you are with them as it is bad for you, as well as them. Individual's might feel that their smoke only affects themselves but every little puff of smoke affects the atmosphere in the long run, as well as other people.

Acid Rain   Acid rain is caused by factories, power stations and vehicles belching out poisonous gases such as sulphur dioxide, nitric oxide and nitrogen dioxide, which rise up into the atmosphere to make acid rain. Children might feel that there is nothing they can do about this state of affairs, as do many adults. They can certainly cut down on car travel, using "Shank's pony" (walking!), cycling on safe tracks and sharing in a car rota system; also, they can have an opinion when it comes to buying or adapting another car, and here their "research" will stand them in good stead.

Experiments with Indicators (Litmus Paper)   Let the children become familiar with using indicator (Litmus) paper by setting up experiments with liquids like lemon juice, milk, rain water, distilled water, tap water. Indicator paper turns red or orange when acid is present as in lemon juice or vinegar, and blue or green with alkalines like milk or bicarbonate of soda solution.

Soil Test for Acid Rain   Collect equal amounts of clay, sandy and chalky soil. Mix a little vinegar with water to make acid rain

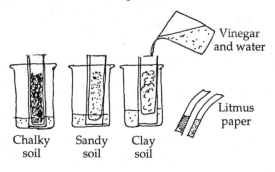

Chalky soil   Sandy soil   Clay soil

Soil test for acid rain

and test the liquid with indicator paper, which should turn red or orange for acid soil and blue or green for alkaline soil. Put filter papers inside three funnels and fill each one with a different soil and stand it in a beaker. Pour some of the acid rain through each funnel of soil and wait for it to drip through into the beakers. Test the water: chalk or limestone soils which are alkaline are good at making the acid weaker, acid soils like clay and loam make the problem worse.

Make Your Own Acid Rain   Buy Campden tablets from a shop that sells ingredients for making wine. Put a crushed tablet into a small jar and pour in a little lemon juice; this produces sulphur dioxide. When the jar is placed in a closed plastic bag with a plant or some leaves, you can see the effect of acid rain. You can compare this with a plant in a plastic bag without the sulphur dioxide. A simpler version of this is to take three similar plants, water one normally, one with a mixture of half-and-half vinegar and water and the third with pure vinegar.

Water

Of all the elements, we are especially drawn to water; it is our energy, our life blood. What could be more attractive to children than a babbling stream to paddle in, or waves of the sea to splash in? Sadly, our water courses and oceans are becoming more and more heavily polluted, and each one of us, adults and children alike, has a part to play in conserving their purity.

"Watch" is engaged in a special research project involving children from eight years old upwards in testing their local water courses for pollution.

Water Activities

Make a Water Filter   The simplest way is to run water through filter paper, which could eliminate some dirt particles. Sand filters can do a little more: fill a fine mesh sieve with a 2" layer of clean fine sand and then the same amount of coarse sand. Pour some dirty water through the sieve and collect it in a white container. Look at it through a magnifying glass; is it cleaner? Alternatively, you can use an upturned plastic bottle as a filter with the base cut off and a double layer of muslin taped over the opening at the neck and then filled with sand. If you can ever visit a waterworks, you will see this process on a grand scale, but it does not eliminate the massive quantities of polluting chemicals which seep through the ground from our houses and factories, and from the pesticides and fertilisers we spread on the land.

Make a water filter

All living beings need to drink water. Have you ever tried to see how long you could manage to go without a drink? Your pets would suffer as much as you would if you forgot to fill their water container. Have you ever found your plants drooping and literally dying for a drink?

Make a Water Clock   Bore a small hole in the bottom of a plastic juice bottle and suspend it over a bowl with two wooden slats. Pour in water with a funnel up to a line where the bottle starts narrowing. Time how long it takes for all of the water to run through and then mark the level at every 10 seconds on a strip of paper stuck on to the whole length of the bottle. Practise timing what you can do in 10, 20 or 30 seconds e.g. how many pats or bounces of a ball.

Fire

Discovering how to make fire must have been the biggest break-through for humanity and it still has compelling fascination for adults and children alike. With restrictions on coal and wood fires, we can be really thankful that the "pea soup" fogs in the big cities are now a thing of the past; but it does mean that today's children have less opportunity of watching the flames and sparks spiral up the chimney. So bonfires and candles have a special role to "keep the home fires burning".

Fire Activities

Making Fire Wearing goggles and gloves, knock two flint stones together and make the sparks fly. This was probably one of the ways in which pre-Stone Age people discovered fire. The Greek myth about Prometheus tells how he brought fire from heaven to give the secret to mortals and was horrifyingly punished for it by the rest of the gods, who felt it should be reserved for them alone.

Fire from the Sun This must be carried out with adults and *great safety precautions*. On a dry sunny day, you can focus the sunlight through a magnifying glass on to tindering material such as fine wood shavings and, when properly focused, it can set alight. As children, we did this in great secrecy amid the hayricks, so it is essential to bring the practice into the open to prevent any risk of fires!

Fire from the sun

It is the same with matches: children will experiment, so it is best to encourage them to learn to strike them when parents are present. They can graduate to lighting candles on the birthday cake, taking care to light the middle ones first and not burning their hands.

Candle Gazing When there is a need to sit quietly for a few minutes, the practice of gazing into a candle flame can be a very calming experience.

Candlelight Candles play a great part in all sorts of celebrations. Have candlelit suppers for any special occasion and enjoy watching the colours and flickering of the flame. At the end of the meal everyone can join in blowing out the candle together with one breath, like the birthday cake ritual.

Candle gazing

Candle Circle In turns, see how fast you can cross a circle with a lighted candle in a wide candlestick, without it going out.

Make Your Own Candles These make very welcome presents and are quite easy to make, but adult supervision is necessary to ensure safety. Warm the wax in a double saucepan and pour into greased moulds – recycled yoghurt pots, milk cartons etc, with a string of wick glued at the base and kept upright in the centre by being attached to a pencil balanced across the top. Different colours can be arranged, letting each one dry first, unless a merging overlap is preferred.

Sand Mould Candles Fill a box with fine, slightly damp sand and push down variously shaped containers to make the mould. Take out the containers and pour in warm wax.

Rainbow Candles　You need blue, red and yellow melted warm wax in tin containers on a stove and a long white candle. You first dip two-thirds of the candle in the yellow wax and dry off for a few minutes. Then you dip the yellow half into the red, leaving a good portion of it still yellow and the rest orange, and the orange end gets an extra dip of red. To get green, you dip the other end into the last part of the yellow leaving the rest blue. A darker blue can be obtained by another dip, and finally the tip of this blue can have a dip into the red to make purple. Supervision is essential throughout and care should be taken not to heat the wax too high.

Candle Smoke　Blow out a candle and place a filter paper to catch the smoke; even one little candle that is burnt sends dirt into the atmosphere. How much more will coal and wood fires and factories?

Enjoying the Sun　There are many ways of appreciating the sun besides sun bathing, which is harmful to our skin especially since the holes in the ozone layer seem definitely to be increasing in size. It is a wonderful experience to greet the sun as it rises and at the same time hear the dawn chorus which in the spring starts just as dawn is breaking. This could be a special family outing with a packed breakfast. A sunset also can be spectacular especially in autumn and calls for a spontaneous picnic in a place where we can see it disappear. So many children have never experienced this twice-daily event, yet it is well worth the effort of getting up at the crack of dawn or finding a viewing place to see the sunset right on the horizon.

Enjoying the sun

Experiments with the Warmth of the Sun

Sun Warmth   We only need to turn our faces to the sun to feel its heat, being careful to keep our eyes closed. We can see how the heat can warm water by placing two bottles of water, one in the sun and the other in the shade, and then taking the temperature of the water in each.

Sun Tea   We can even make tea with the heat of the sun although, as it does not boil, it has to be iced tea. Put a tea bag in a clear glass jar and fill it with cold water and put the lid on. Leave it for at least an hour or two in the hot sun; pour the water over ice cubes and add a little sugar or honey.

A Solar Barbecue   Make a "cooker" from a large cornflake packet and cut half of its side out to make it look like a doll's cradle. Line the whole of the inside of the cooker with aluminium foil and thread a piece of wire through the length of the packet, having first loaded it with pieces of mushroom, apple, tomatoes, pineapple, etc. Place it for the whole day in the full sunlight with the open end facing the sun, turning the wire from time to time. This is a safe experiment for the children to organise themselves and can only be attempted on a really hot day!

Sun Dried Fruit   Cut various fruits into thin slices, dry them and place on a glass dish and cover with muslin. After a whole day in direct sunlight, the fruit should be ready. If you want to make raisins, do the same procedure with a bunch of grapes. Sliced and cored apples and pears can be strung on a taut wire, without touching each other, to get the same result. This could be a reason for a little snack party; can they identify the various sun dried fruits when they are blindfolded?

A Reflector Mobile   Cut out different shapes of aluminium foil and glue them to thin card. String them on to a piece of bamboo, taking care to get the correct balance and hang the mobile near a sunny window.

Sun Prints   Collect a variety of natural items such as flowers, leaves, ferns, feathers etc. Then place them on brightly coloured sugar paper in an artistic pattern and leave them exposed to direct sun for as long as possible. The result will be a delicate print, outlining the parts that have not been faded by the sun.

Make a Sundial   Make a circle out of white cardboard and fix a straight stick about 9 inches long in the middle. Choose a place in the garden which has sunshine all day long and push the end of the stick into the soil. Draw a line along the shadow made by the stick at every hour and write in the time at the end of each line. The shortest line will be at noon and to tell the time point the noon line to the north and then see what time the shadow is pointing to. A more professional sundial would have a triangle of card glued at 45 degrees on to the dial, with its point toward the north.

Make Your Own Compass   Prepare a needle, stroking one half with one end of a magnet and the other half with the other end. Then run the needle through the side of a wide cork and float it in a bowl of water.

Night Sky

Beneath the Stars   Choose a warm summer's night and take sleeping bags and ground sheets to spend some time gazing up into the sky. When there is a full moon, the whole of the garden

Beneath the stars

will be transformed into silvery forms. In autumn the harvest moon will look bigger and ochre coloured and is a beautiful sight when it is full. When there is little moonshine the stars will appear brighter and you will be able to identify some of the constellations: Orion, with its belt of three bright stars, the Plough pointing to the north star and the dog star, Sirius. For safety reasons this activity should be confined to your own garden or that of a neighbour.

Stargazing at the Planetarium   This can be a family visit and then the children might like to put on their own 'Sky at Night' show. They could bore tiny holes at the bottom of large tins in the shape of some of the constellations and project them on to a bare wall with a torch inside each tin.

The Umbrella Night Sky   An old black umbrella could serve as the night sky, with well-known constellations drawn in white chalk with tiny holes pierced to let the light through. They could add even tinier holes to give the impression of myriads of other stars, and a strong light beaming down on the open umbrella could give the children huddling underneath a night sky experience. Alternatively a strong torch inside the umbrella could throw a 'sky at night' shadow on the wall. Older children could be more accurate and draw the main constellations to scale, pointing the centre of the umbrella to the north star as a reference point. They could put up the marked umbrella every month in the same place and see how the stars appear to move, whereas it is the earth itself that is moving.

The Weather

In the old days people would rely on ancient wisdom to foretell the weather. Now most families depend on the daily forecasts. There is a story of some people who went every day to ask a venerable Indian chief what the weather would be. This worked well until one day he said he could not foretell; his radio had broken down!

How reliable are the forecasts from the media? How accurate are the old sayings? The family could test them out. How many

sayings can they think of? A few will be included here under
the various weather headings.

Rain   Try to have some sort of rainwater butt or container in
the garden, balcony or courtyard; your indoor plants will appreciate this, especially azaleas and hydrangeas. You can measure
the rainfall by putting out a large bottle with a ruler stuck to it
and funnel on top to catch the water.

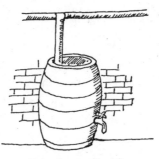

Rain (water butt)

Rainstorm   This is an activity best performed by adults: You
hold a tin tray of ice cubes over the steam of a boiling kettle
and, if possible to arrange, let the condensed water fall on a
thirsty indoor plant.

Sayings: Red sky at night, shepherds' delight.
            Red sky in the morning, shepherds' warning.
            Rain before seven, fair before eleven.

Rainbows   Let's Make a Rainbow: There is something quite
magical about seeing a rainbow. Wordsworth wrote:

> My heart leaps up
> When I behold
> A rainbow in the sky

Children can paint rainbows and make them out of plasticine.
They can hold a prism up to the sunlight or any piece of cut
glass. They can create a rainbow with the spray of a garden
hose by standing with their back to the sun and spraying a fine

mist in front of them against a dark background. They can put a glass of water, filled to the brim, in bright sunlight on the window sill. It should project a little over the inside ledge. They then place a white sheet of paper on the floor below, where the sunshine is focused and a rainbow is created.

> Rainbows at morn
> Good weather has gone
> Rainbows at noon
> Good weather comes soon
> Rainbow at night
> Good weather in sight.

Rainbows

They say that if red is the brightest colour in the rainbow spectrum, it indicates heavy rain; but if the rainbow comes and goes quickly, it means that the rain will soon pass over. It is easy to remember the colours of the rainbow by memorising 'Richard Of York Gave Battle In Vain'. The first letters give the colours – red, orange, yellow, green, blue, indigo, violet.

Thunderstorms These can be frightening and when we were children our fears were allayed by learning to count slowly from the time the lightning flashed to when we heard the thunder, which showed us how far away the eye of the storm was. We calculated a mile for every second and believed it implicitly!

Hailstones Did you know that hailstones are formed by being tossed about in thunderclouds, forming layers of ice? If you are able to capture a hailstone and cut it open you can see the layers.

Clouds Perhaps you can predict the weather better by watching the clouds than by relying on the forecasts. We all know that the darker the thunder clouds are the more likely it is to rain and that the more space between the fluffy white clouds the less chance of rain. Did you also know that wispy clouds high in the sky can be signs of rain?

Most of us have played the game of spotting clouds that look like animals on a fine windy day. They change their shape so rapidly that we can imagine one creature after another riding the sky.

Besides painting clouds with little sponges dipped in white or grey paint, you can also make collages of landscapes with cloud formations made from cotton wool.

The Wind

Pin Wheels These are easy to make with a square of stiff paper or thin card that can be painted with bright colours. Fold the square in both diagonals and cut along the folds to one inch of the centre. Take each corner of the square and fasten it to the centre with a ball headed pin. Make a tiny paper tube $1/2$" long and put it round the pin. Then fix the point of the pin into a rubber at the end of a long pencil. The pin wheel should spin in the wind but if it gets stuck, ease the hole made by the centre pin.

Make a Kite that Flies The familiar diamond shape is an ideal starter kite for children. You can make it out of gift wrapping paper 36" x 36", and split bamboo cane about 36" long and $3/4$" thick, fine cotton twine and enough paper and string for the tail. Split the bamboo down its length, following the grain and using a twisting motion. If this is too difficult to manage you can use $1/2$" cane whole.

The vertical cane should be 36" long and the horizontal one 32" and they are positioned so that the horizontal crosses the vertical 12" from the top. Lash the spars together with damp cotton twine and fix with resin glue. Cut out the sail cover, making folds all round the edges and fasten it to the frame with cotton twine and glue. Fix the twine to the two ends of the vertical spar and join as shown in the illustration. Fasten the string tail to the end of the vertical spar and tie on the paper bows.

So many kites, both homemade and commercial, are destined never to fly properly, but this simple one has proved its worth down through the ages!

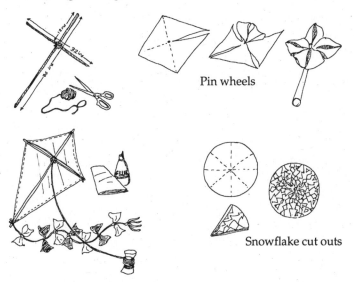

Pin wheels

Snowflake cut outs

Make a kite that flies

Snow   Make the most of snow when it settles as it can be quite short-lived and increasingly rare. In fact we can ask whether the planet is getting warmer because of the greenhouse effect. It is easy to imagine the delights of perpetual summer days, whereas in reality it would be more likely to be perpetual rain and no snow!

Snow Building   What about making a snow woman or a snow castle decorated with treats for the hungry birds – peanuts, dried fruit? Snow animals larger than life, like lions or seals are also fun to make. An igloo would be more ambitious with large bricks, of snow packed into rectangular or square containers used as moulds. They are built overlapping each other so that they gradually form a dome, with the last one supported by the pressure of the adjoining blocks.

Lying in the Snow   If the adults agree, children could experience a few minutes of lying deeply in the snow, wearing old raincoats!

Measuring Snowfall   Use a large tin can and, when full, calculate that 5" of snow equals $^1/_2$" rain.

Making Snow Ice Cream   Mix cream and sugar and some snow and put it in a tin inside a larger tin, packed with snow. Put it outside for a few hours buried in the snow until it is frozen hard.

Catching a Falling Snowflake   Take a container of ice cubes from the freezer and wrap over it a piece of black velvet and hold it out to catch some falling snow – the flakes will retain their shape long enough to be examined under a microscope or magnifying glass or to be photographed. You could also use a sheet of black sugar paper, chilled in the freezer. To make a permanent record of snowflakes, capture them on a pane of glass sprayed with artist's fixative, both chilled until the last minute in the freezer.

Snowflake Cut Outs   Snowflakes always have six sides, so if you fold a paper circle (traced around a plate) in half, and then each half into thirds and then cut patterns when still folded, you can make a whole variety of shapes.

Chapter VI

Enjoying Nature in the Wider World

Although there is now less access to the open country, there are many more opportunities to visit wildlife reserves and nature trails than ever before and if we give our support to the Ramblers' Association in their campaign to keep the footpaths open, everyone will benefit by the access to fields, heaths and woods which is our rightful heritage.

This chapter concentrates on trees to begin with as they are to be found everywhere, in the urban as well as the rural areas, in spite of the fact that they are being felled by the thousands. In the same way all sorts of creatures make their habitats in built-up areas; in trees, bushes and even walls. Ponds and streams may be further afield in commons, parks or heaths and there are still many old village ponds to dip into. We are inclined to forget the possibilities of graveyards, but they are now the guardians of much wildlife and can be a fruitful source of exploration.

Nature in the wider world calls for family outings, not only to the countryside and the sea, but also to nature reserves and sanctuaries for threatened wildlife. These more recent ventures are often organised by the local councils and can be free of charge or with a small entrance fee, and there are now quite a number of farms that cater for visitors, especially families with children, also centres that provide creative activities for children in the realm of nature; for example, butterfly pavilions, nature trails, bird hides and otter reserves.

Trees   Trees are wonderful, they provide food and homes for a host of living creatures including ourselves; they breathe in carbon dioxide, thus easing the dangers of global warming, and they breathe out oxygen, which is what all living creatures need.

Climb a Tree   All children love climbing trees and they usually know how not to take undue risks, although it is better if there is an adult around, as getting down can be daunting. I recall having to be rescued by my father as he rode around the farm on his old grey mare!

Make a Tree Den   One of the most exciting things about playing in trees is to have one's own tree house. This is very much of a luxury, although some parents have managed to compromise by building a 'house' at the base of a tree or even on a water tank, which has access to a tree that will not support a house.

Make a tree den

Dens in the Bushes   If we are not lucky enough to have a tree which could support a tree house in the garden, we can make dens in the bushes in the parks or commons. Making homes is such a basic instinct in young children that it is worthwhile to take them to some places where they can play undisturbed, even if it means that we have to hover nearby for safety reasons. We can also ensure that any litter is carefully collected and disposed of afterwards.

Adopt a Tree   It is fun for children to adopt a tree of their own choice; it should be nearby so that they can explore it with many different activities. They can make rubbings of its bark and take photographs of its changes throughout the seasons and paint a frieze of its varying colours. Some children have a photograph taken every year on their birthday standing against their tree. They can measure their height each time and also measure the height of the tree.

Adopt a tree

How Tall is Your Tree?   You can measure your tree by having a photograph of yourself standing in front of it, making sure that the whole tree is included. Then see how many times your own height will go into the height of the tree on the photograph. Then all you have to do is multiply that number by your present height.

How Old is Your Tree?   You can get an idea of its age by measuring its girth if it has reached maturity, allowing one inch for every year of growth. If you choose a poplar tree, add on some years as it grows quite fast and likewise subtract some for the horse chestnut as it grows more slowly. If you have adopted a pine tree you can count the number of rows or twirls of branches radiating from the central trunk, each row representing a year's growth. Where a tree has been sawn down you can count the rings, each representing a year's growth and you can even find out what kind of year it has been for the tree: wide rings indicate strong growth and narrow ones where the tree had experienced hard conditions.

How old is your tree?

Plant a Tree   As so many trees are being destroyed it is good to try to plant a tree and one of the easiest ways is to dig up a seedling (with permission!) which has self-seeded under a parent tree. Plant it in a large flower pot in good compost. If it thrives then the decision has to be made as to where to plant it more permanently. It will need special care and possibly permission to settle it in a public place. This will be a service to the community as well as to much wildlife.

Cuttings from Trees   Poplars, willows and hawthorn are quick to grow. Pull off twigs at the heel and grow in water or potting soil. Be prepared for failure and keep trying you will certainly succeed in the end.

Cuttings from trees (willow)

Capturing Creatures

If you want to capture creatures from the wild for a day or so, you need to provide accommodation for them: a terrarium adapted from an old aquarium is ideal; otherwise large sweet bottles with gauze or muslin over the lid can be used for temporary shelter. Make sure that there is food available, usually in the form of the plant they were found on, stuck in a jar of water with the opening covered with plasticine or muslin.

First Catch Your Creature   Ground dwelling insects can be trapped in large glass jars sunk in the earth and baited with scraps of food. Prop a board a couple of inches over it with stones, so that the rain does not drown them. You might catch millipedes, springtails, earwigs, ants and beetles.

First catch your creature

Creatures in Leaf Litter   Collect some rich, damp leaf litter and put it in a funnel, which is placed over a glass jar. Shine a hanging lamp over it for a few hours and the insects will be driven down the funnel into the jar, where you can examine them with a magnifying glass before releasing them.

Creatures in leaf litter

Make a Sweep Net You need a bamboo cane, nylon netting or tights and a wire coat hanger twisted into a rectangular or circular shape. Straighten the hook of the coat hanger and tape it to the bamboo; then cut out the netting and tights to fit round the circumference of the wire and tape it, sewing the base and sides of the netting to form a bag. This net can be used for catching insects in the long grass and also for flying insects, twisting the handle when something is caught, so that it cannot easily escape. It is specially exciting to go out at night and attract nocturnal insects with a sheet lit up by a torch. We should remember that all flying insects are extremely delicate and that it is right to release them immediately after observing them.

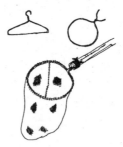

Make a sweep net

Robin's Pincushions These are attractive red and green fuzzy growths containing little grubs found on the stems or leaves of the wild rose. Collect a gall cushion in early spring and keep it in a jam jar until the gall wasps come out. Then release them in a wild rose bush for more robin's pincushions.

Marble Galls These are commonly called oak apples. Collect some and put them in a container so that you can observe the insects when they come out in the autumn. Cut it in two and see how they have got out.

Wildlife Detectives

A favourite activity when in the countryside is to see how many traces of animal wildlife children can find. They can look in the trees, old logs and fallen leaves, and they can track footprints and discover evidence of where animals have been feeding.

Wildlife in the Trees   What about exploring how much wildlife a tree can support? Oak trees seem to be the favourites in housing creatures and a well tried method is to put an umbrella or an old sheet under the tree and to shake the branches above vigorously. A surprising number of creatures will fall down and after looking at them through a magnifying glass you hope that they can climb or fly back to where they came from!

Wildlife in the trees

Wildlife in an Old Log   An old log placed at the foot of a tree will provide a home for many 'creepy crawlies', especially if the log is going rotten. An interest in them might dispel any tendencies to be squeamish, and sometimes it helps to suggest that children should try to find something nice to say about each one: for example a daddy long legs, a spider or a snail.

Spiders and their Webs   Spiders' webs look at their best in autumn when they sparkle with dew drops. If you find a web that is inhabited by a spider, tickle very gently one of the outer strands with a paintbrush and see if the spider comes out to catch its 'prey'. You can see which are the sticky threads which trap the flies by spraying a disused web gently with water. If you would like to make a replica of the real thing, you can transfer an old web to black sugar paper that has been sprayed with hairspray and held against the web immediately afterwards; and to make the threads stand out you can give the web a puff of talcum powder before transferring it. An alternative is to try to make a web yourself with coloured cotton on card with pins to mark where the strands would go. Spiders make the framework of the spokes first and then weave the rings round them.

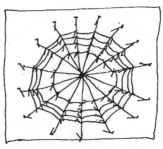

Spiders and their webs

Feather Detectives   Birds release their feathers continually and shed their old ones, so you have a good chance of finding them on the ground. You can tell if they are tail feathers as the shaft runs exactly down the middle, whereas all the others have shafts that are slightly off centre. The soft fluffy down feathers are from the breasts of the birds and some, including owls, actually pluck some of these from their own breasts to line their nests.

Tail feather

Feather detectives

Preening Feathers   Birds spend much of their time preening their feathers, which enables them to keep their beautifully stream-lined contours; in fact, all their feathers with the exception of the tail plumage are called contour feathers. You too can preen the feathers you have collected, (except the fluffy breast ones), by separating the barbs and then joining them together by gently squeezing them between your first finger and thumb.

Animal Tracks   These are easy to trace when they are made in soft ground or snow; you can even tell if the animal was running or walking by measuring the distance between them. Bird tracks can indicate whether they are hoppers or runners: for example, robins hop and crows run.

Casting Tracks   You can make casts of any tracks using a mould of plaster of Paris. You cut rings out of large milk cartons, or glue 1" strips of cardboard to form rings of the size required and insert one round each track. Make a small amount of plaster of Paris and pour it to fill the ring. After about 15 minutes it will have set and you can then dig it up and clean it. You then have raised prints of the track and you can press them into a sheet of clay to make the original imprints, or you can use them raised to make further tracks in the mud.

Casting animal tracks

Animal Track Game   In pairs one player uses cast prints of animals that his partner will try to trace. Besides making casts, they could improvise prints using twigs for bird tracks and clay models for animals and even their own hands bunched to imitate the pads of rabbits or foxes. The illustrations will provide authentic tracks of some of the most likely animals to imitate: for example squirrels, foxes, deer, cows, horses, dogs. The tracks could lead to the creatures' imaginary home: a hole, a nest or a hide out. The player could try to put themselves into the skin of the animal either literally wearing masks, or metaphorically: where would it be likely to go? What would its fears be? The players fears might be that their own footsteps might easily be traces; so they might choose pathways where they themselves could walk on brushwood or dry grass with the animals' simulated footprints in the mud.

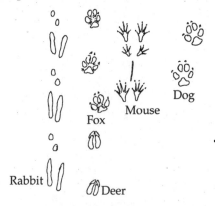

Animal track game

Animal Detectives   Look for any traces of where animals have been: deer may have ripped the bark off trees and nipped buds from the branches. You may find owl pellets under the trees or in barns and if you soak them in warm water, you can dissect the remains of small birds and mammals with a needle or tweezers. Look for animal's holes and signs of earth being dug away. Are there remains of food, skeletons or feathers, or food hordes? For example, jays collect lots of acorns and stack them near a landmark, like a tree, so that they will know where to find them. Make sure that you wash your hands thoroughly afterwards.

Food from the Wild   As children, we were always on the look out for something to eat from the wild, although we were always well fed with good country cooking. In fact, we had a secret little club called "L.F." (The Little Feast Club)! We called the tiny new leaves of the hawthorn tree "Bread and Butter", but I thought there was little resemblance. We would go nutting, mushrooming and blackberrying in the autumn, and we would manage to collect some wild chestnuts in time to roast them on November the 5th. There was also a prolific walnut tree in the glebeland of the vicarage, which covered us with stain as we collected them!

Today, one would have to get permission from the owners to gather wild food such as nuts, berries and fungi, but there are still plenty of commons, heaths and roadside areas where wild herbs can be found. Nettles are everywhere and, wearing gloves, you can pick the youngest leaves to make nettle soup, with onions and cream; in fact nettles might already be established in your butterfly garden. Dandelions are even more common than nettles, and the very young leaves make a tasty salad with an oil and lemon dressing and a sprinkling of the florets for decoration. They can also be served with crispy fried bacon – what the French call "pissenlit au lard"! You can even grow continual supplies of young dandelion leaves by digging up a few roots from the garden and potting them in moist compost and leaving them in a cool, dark place in the house covered with some tissue paper. Dandelion coffee is made by drying the roots in the autumn, roasting them in the oven until they are crisp enough to crumble, and then grinding them in a coffee grinder.

The wild herbs are not as plentiful as they used to be, but wild thyme and marjoram or oregano can still be found in some quantity on the hill pastures and they make fragrant additions to any savoury dish or salad. If you can identify watercress in a clean running stream, it is best to make soup with it, rather than eat it raw in salads, so that there is no risk of any contamination from liver fluke, as the cooking kills the fluke.

Food from the wild

Wild Food Feasts   It would be fun to have a family wild food meal, starting with nettle or watercress soup, then creamed field mushrooms with herbs, dandelion salad, blackberry crumble and hazel nuts as an autumn feast.

The Joys of Exploring Ponds and Streams

Pond Dipping   If you haven't the possibility of making your own mini-pond, you can made an expedition to a nearby pond or stream. You can make a net to go dipping with an old kitchen sieve attached to a long bamboo garden cane, or fashion a wire clothes hanger to the shape desired, circular or rectangular, and sew on a net made out of the foot of an old pair of tights or closely-woven curtain netting, and attach it to the stick by thin wire. In your catch, you could hope to find caddis fly larvae camouflaged with tiny stones and tubitex worms at the bottom of the pond, snails in water weeds and you can gently skim the surface for pond skaters, whirling beetles and mosquito larvae. The catch can be examined by emptying it into a large plastic container and, unless you have an aquarium all set up with the right kinds of plants, you should return the creatures straight away after viewing them.

A Fishing Net Made Out of the Toes of Old Stockings

For minute creatures remove the toe and secure a small jar at the end of it with elastic or string. Examine these creatures under a microscope. You could also use a tea strainer over the base with a large rubber band and you can lower it into the pond and look through the open end. You may see pond snails, water shrimps, water spiders and small fish like minnows, gudgeons or stickle-backs. You will not need your viewer to see the beautiful turquoise dragon and damsel flies settling on their perches, nor the pond skaters gliding over the surface. Streams are wonderful to paddle in; as a child, I could never resist this pleasure, although it was strictly forbidden, owing to my propensity to catch cold on such occasions, which was mostly because I always managed to fall in!

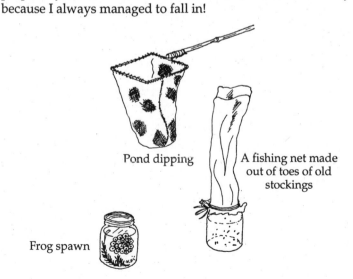

Pond dipping

A fishing net made out of toes of old stockings

Frog spawn

Testing a Pond for Pollution   Apart from the tests of the pond water for toxicity you can be guided by the presence of the pond creatures. If the mayfly is there it is a good sign of clean water; whereas fresh water shrimps can support a little pollution; if only woodlice and bloodworms can be found there must be quite a lot of pollution; and finally if only slugworms or the rat-tailed maggot are present, the pond is very polluted indeed. You could get a book from the library to identify your catch and diagnose the extent of the pollution.

Tadpoles in Your Pond   Look in ponds or streams for frogspawn and take just a small amount in a jam jar with pond weed and some algae. Keep them in an aquarium with pebbles and some large stones and a floating log. You can watch the hind legs and then the front legs emerge and the tail disappear. The tadpoles eat pond weed at first and then can appreciate tiny scraps of meat lowered on a piece of cotton, as do the little frogs. At this stage it is important to cover the top of the aquarium so that they do not jump out, and to make sure that they can reach the rocks above the water level. It is now time to take them back from where they came or to release them near your own homemade pond.

The Seashore

A Litter Drive on the Seashore   Take plastic bags and see how many objects you can pick up that might cause a danger to animals. Six pack rings are a special threat to sea birds such as gulls and when they get washed out to sea, fish and young seals tend to swallow them, mistaking them for sea anemones.

Seaside Creatures   To observe sea creatures, catch them as the tide is going out and keep them for a short time in a jar or bucket with sand. Look for barnacles settled on small stones and put them in a plastic container with sea water and watch them open their shells and push out their little limbs to comb the water for food. Use your water viewer to discover the life in a still rock pool; you may spot some hermit crabs moving across the bottom of the pool. For cockles, you should fill the container half full with sand and top it up with seawater. They will keep in the sand but will put two tubes just above the sand and will siphon off drops of gravy that you can supply with an eye dropper.

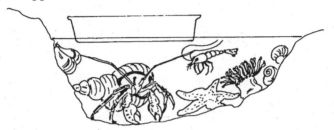

Seaside creatures and viewing box in rock pool

A Salt-Water Aquarium   Children who live near the sea might consider a salt-water aquarium, changing the sea creatures after a brief stay. It would need a lot of sand for cockles, razor shells and tellins, small rocks for barnacles and limpets and plenty of water for the sea anemones.

Collecting on the Seashore   The seashore is a collector's paradise. Shells can be made into models: "crabs" from cockles, "insects" with mussel wings and "boats" from the slipper limpet. They can also be used to make necklaces and brooches, if adults help to bore the holes. Attractive jewel boxes can be fashioned by sticking a variety of tiny shells on to a large matchbox.

Seaweeds   Different seaweeds can be collected and dried, pressed between thick wads of newspaper, and made into a

Seaweeds

collage. My great treat was to see how many bladder wracks I
could pop!

Seaside Mobile   So many delicate sea treasures lend themselves to mobiles, with skate egg cases, periwinkle and tellin
shells and dried seaweed hanging on a piece of driftwood, or
a set of chimes made out of long razor shells.

Through the Diving Mask   Whether you are viewing a rock
pool or swimming in a clear sea, a diving mask can be a reve-
lation into a new world of seaweeds, sea moss, sea lettuce and
grass kelp all shimmering in the reflected light.

Family Outings   Besides the numerous activities of the
organisations concerned with the conservation of nature as
listed in the appendix, there are traditional visits to zoos and
museums.

A Visit to the Zoo   There is a great debate taking place about
the role of zoos: some saying that it is cruel to keep the animals
in cages and others that this is the only way to breed endangered
species. As with most discussions of this kind, the happy
medium seems to make sense: where possible animals need the
maximum space, safari style and it is good to see them in
something nearer to their natural habitat; on the other hand
there might well be a case for some smaller units concentrating
only on breeding, which is often hard to achieve results.

Children will have opinions on this and often their sympathy
goes out to the animals prowling backwards and forwards the
length of their cages. As with all institutions, small is beautiful
and, if numbers of small specialised zoos were the order of the
day, outings to them would be more accessible and the animals
would have more space.

Design a Cage   Some children might like to try their hand
at designing a more humane cage, with shelter, privacy and
space to move about; others might feel that they could only
agree to planning a safari park, presumably with unlimited
money!

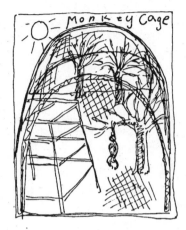

Design a cage

Animals in Cages This is a 'pretend' game for young children. Each child has a hoop and chooses to be an animal at the zoo. The 'keeper' wakes them up and feeds them and they take some exercise round the hoop and then they sleep at night. Some players could act as visitors and stare at them, making fun of them and giving them the wrong kind of food. They could then talk about how they felt.

Action in the Wider World

Throughout the book there have been suggestions for action to conserve the natural world as well as merely enjoying it. Families that have practised ecological approaches both in the home and their outside environment will be specially aware of the need to extend their activities to the community and the wider world. Fortunately there is a plethora of organisations both general and specific, that will give practical guidance on how they can best contribute. A number of these have special sections for young people, with or without their families. Two of the most active of these are the Young Ornithologists Club, and Watch, the Wildlife and Environmental Club for Young People.

It is not within the scope of this book to give details of all of the pressure groups and organisations that cater for the conservation of the environment, (the addresses of an appropriate section of these are listed in the appendix) so here is information about the ones that would specially appeal to parents and their children. It is really heartening to realise how much activity is now taking place, ranging from the protection of whales to hedgehogs, rainforests to hedgerows and also many groups that are trying to turn the tide against pollution.

The Centre for Alternative Technology runs courses for young people, giving them hands on experience of renewable energy supplies and organic waste disposal.

The Children's Scrapstore is a national recycling scheme set up by the Federation of Resource Centres, providing all sorts of materials from industry, which can be recycled for children's play and recreation. They also hire out larger items such as tents and minibuses and give workshops and training.

The City Farms National Federation gives information about the growing number of city farms which have sprung up in many urban areas. Most of them concentrate on animals that will specially appeal to children, such as goats, rabbits, sheep, donkeys, pigs, and parties of children are specially welcome.

Common Ground has been organising a Parish Maps Project in which children play an important role in charting what specially appeals to them in the local countryside. The maps of the locality can be made in many forms: pictures, performances and even quilts. Other projects include, 'Trees, Woods and the Green Man'; 'Save our Orchards' and it promotes festivities during the celebrations of the solstices and also the new celebration of Apple Day and Tree Dressing Day. It has a wide selection of posters, cards and T-shirts for sale and also exhibitions for hire.

Commonwork is a green education centre in Kent which provides children with imaginative and unforgettable experiences such as milking cows, making jam, yoghurt and bread, digging clay and making clay stoves, also their own shelters from biogradable materials. In these activities they become more aware of the survival techniques practised by many peoples in the Third World.

Earth Action is the youth section of Friends of the Earth which provides a focus for local groups of young people aged between 14 to 23 to campaign on environmental issues. On Earth Action Day, January 28th, they warn the public on the dangers of global warming. They also campaign on such issues as saving the whale and the need to recycle.

Keep Britain Tidy has a youth action pack for the 8 to 14 year olds with ideas for lots of activities.

The National Council for Clean Air can provide a set of illustrated fact sheets for 9 to 12 year olds on pollution and gives information about experiments that can be carried out, and also field studies.

The National Trust has a youth section which issues an exciting quarterly magazine for its members, giving ideas for activities and many of its sites provide special programmes for children such as guided walks, creative projects and role play in prehistoric buildings. There is also a Young National Trust Theatre which produces shows for children on 'living history'.

The Pedestrians Society campaigns to make roads safer for walkers; it lobbies Parliament and publishes the magazine 'Walk'.

The Young Ornithologists Club is the junior section of the Royal Society for the Protection of Birds for young people between the ages of 8 to 14, although younger and older members are welcome. There is a lively colour magazine 'Bird Life', which is sent six times a year, over 100 RSPB nature reserves to visit, exciting projects on action for birds and all sorts of outings and holidays, organised by local groups. Family membership is encouraged and the area of interest has been greatly expanded to include all sorts of wildlife and particularly that which is threatened.

The RSPB Action for Birds is for all age groups: youth clubs, school classes and individual families. There is a system of credits: 50 for bronze, 150 for silver and 250 for gold awards. For example, birdtables, nestboxes, bat boxes, newly created score 5 points, as do searches for litter and clearing of an abandoned fishing line, also the planting of a tree or shrub. Visits to nature reserves and trails and organising a conservation display and creating a wild patch all earn 10 points. Detailed instructions on all of the tasks are available from the RSPB, with emphasis on conservation and the nurturing of wildlife. They have also produced a booklet: 'Environmental Games Guide' for outdoor group activities: for example, team races with players picking up food wearing kinds of beaks; role play as wardens with decisions to make; an estuary game with cards drawn to indicate loss of birds because of rubbish tipping, fish farms, pollution, etc.

The Royal Society for the Prevention of Cruelty to Animals has a junior membership for children under 17 years of age.

The Royal Society for the Prevention of Accidents produces a 'Green Cross Guide' to help children cope with road traffic hazards. The 'Tufty Club' provides books and games to teach children of 3 to 7 years old and their parents about safety in the home, on the roads and near water. It also organises the National Bike Club for young cyclists and their families to help them to stay alive on the road.

Watch is the junior section of the Royal Society for Nature Conservation and it organises projects that children can participate in, such as 'Acid', which was an award-winning survey of rainfall acidity. Children tested the rainfall daily over a period of time and with over 20,000 of them taking part, a national survey of the amount of acid in the rain was compiled. There have also been activities on recycling, bumblebee walks, surveys on dragon flies and barn owls. 'Ladybird Spot' was a survey of Britain's ladybirds and led to the discovery of a species of two spotted ladybird, which was thought to be extinct. 'Battitudes' researched people's attitudes towards bats and as they are in danger of becoming extinct, it helped people to appreciate the work that the bats do in consuming enemy insects.

The present research, always carried out by children, is 'Watch on Streams' which gives an opportunity to monitor stream pollution at a local level, using a specially developed 'slide rule'.

All of these activities involve children in their own right and their work illustrates how much they can contribute to the care of the natural world. Individual children and their families can belong to Watch; they receive the club magazine, and can work for badges which are given for active involvement in protecting the environment.

The Young Vegetarians are part of the Vegetarian Society and they campaign for acceptable and healthy vegetarian meals at school. The Vegetarian Society also promotes SCREAM, which stands for the School Camp Against the Cruelty of Factory Farm and Slaughter-houses. There are also two other vegetarian clubs and both of them campaign for vegetarianism with magazines and badges: The 'Green Gang' for the under twelves and 'Vegetarians First' for the twelves to eighteens.

Chapter VII

Nature Games

This chapter deals with a wide range of games that are all connected with nature in some way. Most of the activities can be enjoyed in the setting of a small family unit or club groups and others are suitable for more players at a celebration, a party or a club. The games are all co-operative in essence and this is particularly important in the family setting, where there is always a wide range of ability amongst the siblings. There is a mixture of indoor and outdoor games with the emphasis on playing in the open air and the repertoire is for all age groups including the adults.

Starting with a word about the benefits of relaxation and visualisation and games of the senses, it goes into more detail with animal guessing games, treasure and litter hunts, blindfold and camouflage games, food chain puzzles, pelmanism and happy family adaptations and finally nature watch games.

Relaxation and Visualisation It could be true that most children do not get enough opportunities to relax completely these days and several ideas have already been suggested, such as lying in a meadow or under a tree and looking upwards at the sky or, in the evening, gazing at the moon and stars.

Visualisation This is something that parents might like to experience with their children, taking them on imaginative journeys over snow-capped mountains, crystal blue seas and then at nightfall visiting the moon. A much more simple but effective approach is to leave much to the children's own imagination, when they find their own secret place, through doors, down steps, along paths to a sanctuary which they can visit whenever they wish and only they know the way.

Games of the Senses

These games are played for fun, but they also convey a deeper observation and understanding of the world around them and the children's senses are sharpened to appreciate the sounds, scents, sight, feel and tastes of all things in nature.

Sense Hunt   Each player goes out to find something that appeals to their senses of sight, touch, smell, sound and taste and then takes turns to lead the others round to share their choices with them. It might be a flower in full bloom, a herb to smell, a pebble to feel and a bird's song to hear. They could play this in the garden or a park, but their sense of taste would have to be curtailed in the wild, (unless they found blackberries or nuts) as they should never experiment with tasting anything unknown.

Sense hunt

Guessing Through Your Senses   There have been sense games throughout this book, spotting wildlife, learning bird calls, and blindfold Kim's game, but the senses of smell and taste have not featured so directly. Favourite smelling and tasting guessing games are usually blindfold with natural items in small bags for the sense of smell, or tiny tasters on cocktail sticks dipped in sugar, salt, flour etc. Tasting sessions are also fun with small pieces of fruit or vegetables to guess.

Animal Games

Animal Partners   Each player picks a card with a picture of an animal and as there are two of each, the game is to find your partner. The popular noisy version is to call out your sound: braying, bleating, mooing, neighing, cackling, grunting, etc. A quiet alternative is to mime your actions and this is far more difficult: frogs, snakes, horses, butterflies, cats and dogs come to mind. The third possibility is to make a statue of yourself as a creature and in this case you would display your stance one by one and at the end see who would pair off. Older children can prepare the cards with cut outs or original drawings.

Animal Groups   The technique of animal partners can be used to get children into groups of certain numbers. This avoids the difficulty of some children being left out. In this case the number of cards for each species would reflect the number required in each group.

Flocks of Birds   This game is on the lines of Animal Partners, but this time it is limited to bird calls, with duplicate pictures of birds given out to players. They have to recognise the bird and know what its call is and their experience with taping birds' songs should stand them in good stead here. The sounds could be practised beforehand. The cuckoo is easy, as is the mallard, or wild duck and the owl. Players might have to learn more unusual calls such as 'pee-ee wit' for the peewit, plover or lapwing; 'Jack, Jack' for the jackdaw; 'Pink, pink' for the chaffinch; 'Teacher, teacher' for the great tit and 'Chatter, chatter' for the magpie. Other interpretations will be different, so it is best to listen and make up one's own words or calls.

Animal Mime   Each player mimes an animal and the rest guess what it is. If they have difficulty, the 'animal' is allowed to make one sound.

Animal mime

Animal Picture Consequences   Each player draws the head of a creature at the top of the page and folds it over and passes it to the next player with just the line of the neck showing. Then the body is drawn with the same procedure and finally the legs and tail.

Animal Consequences   Every character must be a creature or a plant in this adaptation of the popular game of consequences.

Invented Animals   Everyone could invent an animal and draw it, and then give it a name and a call. There could be great variations in character. A monster, an undiscovered dinosaur, a mixture between different species, possibly inspired by Animal Consequences.

Nature Charades   Play charades in the usual way, but the words must be animals, (alternatively plants), eg kitten, dandelion, chestnut, walnut, etc. The drama can be mimed or spoken.

Big Snake   Wearing old clothes the children begin by lying stretched out on the floor or grass and then connect with each other by wriggling along until they can hold on to each other's ankles and form a long snake.

Centipede   The players form a line, all facing in the same direction. The first two have their right feet tied together and the second and third their left feet and so on. Can they now crawl like a centipede?

Rabbits   One person sits in the middle of the 'rabbit' circle and points to one of the rabbits, who must immediately 'waggle his ears' with his hands and those immediately on either side of him must do the same with their hand that is nearest the one waggling. This is a version of the popular, 'Elephant and Palm Tree', and children can have fun making up new ones, like, 'Butterfly', with two antennae in the middle and wings at either side; or 'Penguin' with head down in the middle and flippers on each side. If anyone gets it wrong they have the privilege of coming into the middle to take the place of the caller and, after a little practice they could call out any of the three creatures; rabbit, butterfly or penguin or any others that they have devised.

Tree Homes   The children each choose to be a creature that lives in trees: owl, wood pigeon, squirrel, tree creeper, dormouse, spider, woodpecker, crow etc. Some children are designated to be trees with their arms outstretched and the others are only allowed to stay in the tree (where they cannot be caught) for 10 seconds, after which they must seek another tree. Two chasers try to catch them in between trees and if a creature is caught it becomes a tree, the tree becomes a chaser and the chaser takes the place of the creature that was caught.

Matching Objects Race   Duplicate pictures of trees, plants or flowers are given out, one for each player and the numbers should be even. They are lined up at a distance from a table where a number of natural objects are lined up to correspond in some way to the pictures: for example, an acorn would match with an oak, a beechnut with a beech tree, a grass seed with a clump of grass, a toothed leaf with a dandelion flower. When the name of their picture is called out the two players who have identical cards race to the table and see who gets the object that corresponds to their picture. When every couple has had a turn the game can begin again.

Guessing Games

What's My Line?   Each player chooses a plant or creature and describes its job, e.g. my job is to protect plants in the garden, such as roses and dahlias. I have a great appetite and can fly from plant to plant. I am not afraid of being attached by bigger creatures that fly as they don't like my taste (one can add more information about ladybirds according to the knowledge of the players: for example, I love to eat aphids). Instead of concentrating on jobs, descriptions of the subject's appearance and habits can be a starting point. This is really a variation of the popular "animal, vegetable or mineral" when pictures or names can be pinned on players' backs and only answers of "yes" or "no" are permitted.

What am I?   This is similar to 'What's my Line?', but it is played with two teams, which can be as small as two in each. The teams decide on a creature and take it in turns to ask a question which the other group answers in terms of 'yes' or 'no'. This is a good family game as there has to be consensus as to the answer.

Guess the Proverb   Think of a proverb concerned with nature and divide into two teams, one to act it out and the other to guess. There could be as few as two in each team. Ideas could be: 'Make hay while the sun shines'; 'Every cloud has a silver lining'; 'Birds of a feather flock together'; 'A bird in the hand is worth two in the bush'; 'A rolling stone gathers no moss'; 'Don't put all your eggs in one basket'; 'Don't count your chickens before they are hatched'; 'It never rains but it pours'; 'It's an ill wind that blows nobody good'.

Guess my Drawing   In pairs one draws a creature or a plant and the other guesses it as it is being drawn. The artist does not speak until the partner has guessed correctly.

Guess my drawing

Guess the Habitat   This could be in the form of a tableau or a mime with groups of three taking part. Some ideas would be: a pond with frogs hopping, reeds waving in the breeze and a goldfish swimming; or the seashore with sand castles being built, the tide coming in and anemones gently opening and closing their tentacles.

Treasure Hunt   We always had a traditional treasure hunt for birthday parties, organised by the older children with clues that rhymed. One important thing to remember is that the clues must be securely fixed; if one is missing it causes chaos (as we discovered!) In a nature treasure hunt, every clue should relate to the natural world: a particular tree or bush, a stream, a rabbit hole, a decaying log, a sandy hollow, etc. The itinerary needs to be carefully planned beforehand and the limits of the park or common well defined. There is an advantage in having a group hunt as the 'pack' keeps together, and no-one is lost. The first one who finds the clue, which might be an anagram or in code, waits until the others have come and then reads it out and they all dash off to the next one.. The treasure can be a little bag of goodies for each one, containing nuts, dried fruit, apples and sweets. A variation is that at each stop for a clue there is a group job to do, like build a faggot house, (with bundles of sticks from pruning supplies); if this is too ambitious, the requirements could be finding six different kinds of grasses, seeds or leaves and bringing them to the final clue for the treasure.

Guarding the Treasure   This is an adaptation of an old favourite, where one person is blindfold and the others try to creep up on him or her without being heard. In this case there can be real treasure to be shared by everyone: fruit, nuts, etc. Played out of doors it is good practice in moving soundlessly. If the guardian hears anyone approaching he points in their direction and they go back to the starting line. Everyone should have a turn at being the guardian before the treasure is eaten.

Foxes and Hen   A variation of guarding the treasure is Foxes and Hen, when the hen is in her house and the foxes have to creep up and tag her. There is a bell placed some way from the hen-house, which they must ring before being able to touch the hen. The hen can order back any foxes she can see approaching, but if there are a number of them all creeping from the bushes this is not so easy. The success of the game depends on the situation of the hen house with bushes around it and the fact that the foxes probably need to co-operate so that one rings the bell while the others have a strategy to advance under cover.

Treasures in a Matchbox   Everyone is given an empty matchbox and is asked to fill it with as many nature treasures as possible. The secret is to seek really tiny items, such as the seed of shepherd's purse, a fallen leaf, a coloured pebble, a beechnut, etc.

Treasures in a match box

Green Games

Recycling Lucky Dip   Make a lucky dip container with wrapping paper tied round the outside and fill it with a number of every-day objects that could be recycled: for example, a tin can (without a jagged edge), a yoghurt pot, a plastic lemonade bottle, a clean piece of foil, a cotton reel, a cardboard cylinder, a cork, etc. The children could parcel them up to disguise their shape and size and everyone takes it in turn to pick out an object and say as many different ways of recycling it as they can think of, counting a point for each agreed use.

Scavenger Hunt   Each player or partners are given a list of natural items to be collected without causing any damage: for example, a dandelion leaf, a diseased leaf, a hazelnut, a funny shaped stone, a strand of hay, wool, a winged seed, a tiny piece of lichen, a dead flower, a bird's nest that has been finished with, a dandelion 'clock', a tiny evergreen leaf, evidence of wildlife etc.

Litter Hunt   This is similar to the scavenger hunt, but the 'litter' has been placed beforehand. It could include such items as plastic six ring holders, bottle tops and ring pulls, paper, rubber bands, crisp bags, cigarette packets, ice cream cartons and spoons, tins, sweet wrappings, receipts, etc. After an agreed time everyone comes to the base and in turns shows one piece of their collection and says what should have been done with it: the tins in the tin bank, cartons for bird 'cakes' etc. Be sure to wear gloves to pick up the litter or use a stick with a wire hook attached with strong glue. Make sure that after you have finished you take *all* the litter with you in a black bag.

Litter hunt

How Green are You?   Players have a questionnaire each, beginning with the words, 'Find someone who ....?' For example, ' who has picked up some litter today, (or yesterday)'; 'who belongs to a Nature Club'; 'who has gone on a nature trail'; 'who has planted mustard and cress'; 'who cleans out the family pet'; 'who feeds the birds in winter'; 'who uses recycled paper'; 'who makes compost in their garden'; 'who has helped to plant a tree'; 'who has made a nest box'. The players write the name of the person who has confirmed his or her action: e.g. Find someone who collects for the bottle bank .... Mary.

Blindfold Games   The favourite is probably still *blindfold partners*, where the blindfold person is led through a maze of natural obstacles: trees, bushes, rocks, streams etc. to reach his special place or tree. Then, after a roundabout route back, he seeks it with the blindfold removed.

Feeling my Rock   Everyone goes out to find a special stone, pebble or piece of rock that they like the feel of. Then all the items are put in a bucket, and each one has to identify his own rock without looking.

Feeling my rock

Dolphin and Fish   Two blindfold players in a circle, one dolphin and one fish with the predator trying to catch its prey. The fish has to keep making a faint rippling noise that the dolphin, owing to its supersonic hearing, can detect. When the fish is caught, two other players take their place. The game 'Bat and Moth' can be played in the same way, with the moth having to make a fluttering noise. Children should know of the danger dolphins are in, as they are continually trapped in the huge nets thrown to catch tuna fish.

Predator Chase   Players take partners and together choose a nocturnal animal: bat, mouse, rat, cat, frog, etc. and decide on their call. Two players are foxes and are out to catch their prey before they link up for protection. The partners are separated, one to each end of the playing space, and the foxes are in the middle. They are all blindfolded and the first couple caught before they meet become foxes, and the original foxes become the animals that were caught.

The Blindman and His Dog   One player is blindfolded and he arranges with his dog a code for communicating such as a whistle, with different messages: for example, one for straight on, two for turn left, three for turn right and a series of quick notes to indicate danger, stop dead. The couple are separated and various obstacles put in between them and the game is to get them together.

Twin Leaves   Distribute a leaf to every blindfold player, making sure that there are two of each kind. Then everyone has to find their partner by feeling the leaves; oak, willow, hawthorn, beech, ash, sycamore, fern and laurel are good choices. Do they know their names? This is one of the many ways to get partners organised without stress as with animal partners.

What Do I Feel?   Sit in a circle with a large blanket covering everyone from the waist downwards and with hands below. The leader passes round, under the blanket, a series of nature objects to be felt and named. If someone does not know it, it is passed on round the circle until someone does identify it. Objects could be various nuts, including acorns and beechnuts, pine cones, all sorts of fruits and seeds, leaves, etc.

Motorway   Each player chooses an animal and they line up on either side of a very wide "motorway", indicated by long sticks. Two players are traffic using the motorway – they can decide whether they are lorries or cars. When an animal's name is called, he crosses the road in his way of moving, e.g. a frog or a rabbit would hop or jump. At the same time, "lorry" or "car", posted further up the motorway, would be called at the same time to drive down and "run over" an animal, and if they catch an animal they change places. This game is a reminder of how many wild animals are deprived of their habitat by motorways and get killed in trying to cross them.

Games in the Dark   There is an eerie thrill about playing out of doors when dusk descends. This is a good opportunity for adults and children to play together, not only for safety reasons but also for that special bond that links us all in the dark.

Night-time Hide and Seek   This is best played along a path or track with players hiding one at a time. They should blend with the bushes and keep very still. Can the seekers sense their presence?

Night-time Follow My Leader   This can be an adventur-ous trek, either by holding the hand of the one in front or keeping in line by means of a rope or thick string that has been prepared beforehand. I recall a trail that took us over a tiny stream, then over the low branches of a tree and finally a steep climb up the stones of an old ruin! I was helped greatly by the one in front of me and I tried to do the same for the one behind. In daylight or at dusk, blindfolds can be worn except for the leader. A blindfold variation is to have a short line of children encouraged by the leader to use all their senses. When they are released and their blindfolds removed can they return to the same place by their sense of smell, touch and hearing?

Night time follow my leader

Caterpillar   Make a tunnel out of an old narrow sheet, knotted at the ends, and get the children to crawl in, holding each other round the waist. At first try with only two children, progress-ing to three and so on. Eyes could be made for the leader and with practice they could crawl over large cushions.

There can be variations of this: tortoise, with a child at each corner of a square cover; crab, with four children walking sideways; and big snakes under a very long narrow cover. (This is one way of using very old draperies and if there are a few holes in them, all the better.)

Camouflage

Spot the Objects   Choose twelve unnatural objects of different shapes and colours and hide them in a small area outside: the garden or the park. Then singly or in pairs the children see how many they can spot in a given time and write them down. It is fun for the children to plan this game and to take some time to find objects that would blend with nature. Even if there are only four players, both couples could have collected their objects previously and they would take turns in hiding them. They could think of coloured wool or cotton, paper, beads, pieces of cloth, a hairpin, a shoelace, a button, etc. The area would have to be designated clearly, especially if the objects were quite small. Another version would be to try to camouflage obvious litter like crisp packets, can rings, plastic and metal, ice cream tubs, etc.

Hidden Animals   Paint or draw a picture where there are animals hidden because of their camouflage. Again this is a puzzle that the older children could design for the younger ones. The easiest creatures for a first attempt would be a family of stick insects!

Camouflaged Animal Masks   First choose what animal you are going to be and make a mask accordingly. Full faces of the cat family, owls, primates and monkeys can be simple paper plates, with elastic bands round the back of the head. The important factor is to colour them to merge with the background you want to hide in: bushes, grass, a hollow tree, sand, a fallen log, etc according to where you can hide. Masks for animals with narrow faces could cover half the face with large openings for eyes and fitting over the nose, or they could be cut out of double card and stapled together. One by one the players can hide and the rest will find them. Small children could be asked to make their animal's noise after a while, to make it easier for them to be found although it will probably be very easy to spot them!

Camouflaged animal masks

Hidden Cocktail Sticks   Hide a quantity of different coloured cocktail sticks and get the players to find as many as they can in a limited time. Which colours were the easiest to find and which the hardest? Play the same game with six inch twigs, cut exactly so that they can be identified. What a difference from the plastic colours!

Dressing-up Camouflage   This is where the children raid the dressing-up box and try to wear things that will hide them in a wooded environment. Green and brown would be in demand and even wrapping paper. Then they play hide and seek.

Food Chain Games

Associations   This is a game literally to keep the ball rolling and to prepare for food chain connections. Players sit in a circle and the facilitator explains that they are going to make a web of associations, preferably ones connected with nature. She starts by saying a word, for example, 'daffodil' and throws a ball of wool to another player, keeping the end firmly in her hand. The receiver has to say a word that she associates with daffodil, for example, 'spring', and throws the ball to someone else, who might say 'Easter', and so on. This activity gives an idea of how much everything is interconnected.

Connections This game starts in exactly the same way as Associations, but this time the players are going to be living plants or animals that are dependent on each other with respect to food chains. The leader might start off with the word 'lettuce' and then throw the ball of wool to someone who must think of a food chain connection with 'lettuce', such as 'slug', who might say 'frog' or 'thrush' and after that it could be a heron who would eat the frog or a cat who might catch the thrush. At this stage both the heron and the cat would finally die and be buried in the ground, so the next person would have to choose to say, 'mother earth' and then the chain could start all over again with a plant. To help the players there could be lists of possible food chains available on cards.

Connections

Poison! This is really a continuation of 'Connections', when after the web has been well established, the leader can say that one item has been poisoned, for example, some herbicide on the lettuce. The lettuce gives a tug on the wool, which affects the slug, which also gives a tug; this continues, and the frog or the heron, also give a tug and this gets us back to mother earth. Meanwhile the affected plant and animals gradually sink down to die and this affects all the rest of the participants with the pulls on the wool. This is a clear example of how everything on earth is interdependent and that herbicides and pesticides affect us all. The poison game can then begin at the beginning with 'Connections' and when everyone is connected by the wool another player can call out 'Poison!' and describe what has happened: it might be that the sea has become polluted or Mother Earth herself, which would lead to a lot of tugging of the wool!

You Need Me, I Need You   This is another interdependence game that can be played out of doors, in a wood or a park. One player has the ball of wool and winds the loose end round his waist and starts by saying that he is a horse chestnut tree and he asks if there is someone who needs him or is needed by him. Another player could volunteer the information that he was a boy and needed the conkers from the tree. The next player could need the conker to plant a new horse chestnut tree. It could continue with compost to plant the conker and someone else requiring the compost for his window box and so on. Each time someone new is introduced the wool is tied round their waist, so that they are all tied to each other. The first player can make a suggestion as to what might damage the web and ask for others to contribute: the tree might be cut down or be uprooted in a gale; it might have a disease and produce no fruit; no-one has managed to make some compost, so the seedling dies. As in 'Poison' any disaster means that the link of the wool must be cut and so gradually the ties are severed.

You need me, I need you

Plants, Creatures and Habitats   Each player has a large circle of sugar paper and draws a plant, a creature and a habitat that they like. Then in turns they make a connection with a crayon from one of their three drawings to another. The circles should be touching, so this is best played on a large table or on the floor. The connections could be quite imaginative: for example, creatures that would fight each other, a plant that would like a certain habitat; an animal that would like to eat a plant. After a few rounds they could each add an extra plant, then next time an extra creature, perhaps a human, and finally an extra habitat. There could be provocative additions like drawing a mouse near a cat, or a whale stranded on the beach, an eagle hovering overhead.

Chain Chase   Each player is given a large sticker with the name of an animal, mini-beast, or plant that feeds on or is fed by other species in the group. The game is to catch your prey without being caught, and the plants have to try to keep hidden as they have no-one to chase. For example, a rabbit chases a cabbage, a fox pursues the rabbit and the huntsman hunts down the fox. Anyone who is tagged changes stickers.

Swallows and Flies   This is one of many chasing games based loosely on parts of the food chain. The swallows wear blue ribbons secured with safety pins and the flies wear white ribbons. When the flies are caught they change roles with the swallows.

Swallows and flies

Goldfish and Tadpoles   This starts in the same way as 'Swallows and Flies', with the goldfish trying to catch the tadpoles and if successful they change ribbons. But there is a secondary predator hovering around in the form of a pike, which is able to attack them both if it catches them just as they are exchanging, and only at that time. Then both the goldfish and the tadpoles become pikes and the pike changes into a tadpole and the game should end up with the pikes being in the majority. The goldfish could wear gold ribbons, the tadpoles green and the pikes brown, with extra brown ribbons provided when the pikes proliferate.

Dragonflies, Frogs and Herons   At first there are only frogs chasing dragonflies in the game, with the dragonflies skimming over the 'water' gracefully and the frogs jumping and hopping. When a frog captures a dragonfly he takes her along with him hand in hand and they have to avoid the heron who has now entered the scene. If the heron catches them he eats them both as the fly is really inside the frog; so they have to join hands and try to catch remaining frogs who might have a dragonfly in tow. A heron would not deign to chase a dragonfly but a frog would be a tasty morsel!

Pelmanism Games   Pelmanism is played by putting all cards face downwards on the table and taking turns to pick two to make pairs. It is a game of memorising.

Animal Pelmanism   Make a set of cards with pairs that match two parts of an animal: for example, one card with an

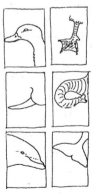

Animal pelmanism

elephant's trunk and another with a tusk; a monkey's face and its tail curling round a branch; a cockerel's comb and its curved tail feathers; a duck's bill and webbed feet; an eagle's upper beak hooked over the lower one and its large curved claws, etc. Much of the fun is in making up the cards: either cutting them out of magazines as part of a jigsaw or painting and crayoning them. A good preparation for this game would be homemade jigsaws of animals in their natural habitats.

Male-Female Pelmanism A simpler version of animal pelmanism is to have pairs of male and female animals cut out from magazines and pasted on cards: for example, lion and lioness; hart and hind; ram and ewe; and for bird lovers, pheasants, blackbirds and mallards all have distinct differences between male and female, with the male having the fine feathers!

Habitat Pelmanism The children could prepare matching cards: one of a habitat, like a pond, a wood, a log or a tree and the other of creatures who would make this area their habitat. There would obviously be some overlapping, but duplicates of habitats could make this an easy game for the younger ones, as there would be more creatures than habitats.

Happy Family Games

Animal Happy Families Make sets of four with the father, mother and two offspring: for example, bull, cow and two

Animal happy families

calves; ram, sheep and two lambs; stallion, mare and two colts.
Play in the usual way of taking turns to ask for what you need
to make sets. A more advanced version would be with animals
or flowers of the same species: eg, the cat family, or the daisy
family.

Food Chain Families   Players are dealt out cards making
sets of four food chain sequences. The game is played like
'Happy Families', asking in turn for cards to make up their set.
In all of the food chain games it is a good idea to have pictures
on view to show the sequence. These could be painted or made
as a collage of cut-outs by the older children, who could collect
more examples of food chains. Easier sets for both of these
games could be restricted to three items: for example, duckweed
– duck – human being; grain – mouse – eagle; plankton – whale
– human being.

I Spy Games   Most of us have resorted to I Spy games when
we are with our children on a long journey. I recall racking my
brains for something unusual and spotting a monkey puzzle
tree! As we drove through that suburban area it seemed that
neighbours were vying with each other in growing monkey
puzzle trees in their front patches. They all had one!

Alphabet I Spy   Each player has a sheet with squares for
each letter in the alphabet. When they spy anything in nature
they write it down in the appropriate square.

Matching Squares   Prepare a sheet of thin cardboard for
each player marked with 2" squares and write in each square
what they should stick in it with sellotape or glue. The finds
would have to fit in the square and the usual rule would be not
to pick anything growing. Your choice would depend on the
locality, but such items as a fallen leaf, a smooth pebble, a twig,
some sand, a seed, a feather, would be common to most areas.
Alternatively you could fill the squares with adjectives: shiny,
rough, dirty, smooth, pointed, soft, sweet smelling, etc. This
game could lead to making nature collages, with all the spaces
in between being filled artistically. Different shaped leaves could

be stuck on to a large card and matched with fallen leaves of the same size and shape. In autumn it could develop into a colour matching game or you could have an array of natural objects with everyone trying to find duplicates.

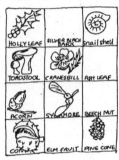

Matching squares

My Special Treasure From Nature   The participants go out into the garden or the countryside and seek for a special treasure from nature. It might be a smooth stone, a winged seed, autumn leaf, a dandelion puff; then each one brings their treasure and says why they chose it.

Stepping Out   In the countryside or a park each player takes turns to cast the dice and takes as many giant strides as the number thrown in any direction. On arriving he identifies something there, either a plant or a creature that he is interested in, and the others carry on from that spot. Each identification must be different and named if possible.

Matching Plants Race   Pictures of trees, plants or flowers are handed out, one card for each player. At the word go, they race to find their plant where it is growing. If there are players who cannot find their plant the others could help them.

Variations of Kim's Game   Show a number of natural items on a tray for one minute and then get the players to find all the equivalents in the wild, or they could paint a picture incorporating as many items as they recall. A blindfold touch variation would be interesting, with conkers, walnuts, shells, leaves, etc.

Chapter VIII

Celebrations and Action

This is a calendar of some of the main festivals and action days for conservation. Celebrations and festivals have always been rooted in seasonal cycles because the lives of human beings have been intrinsically linked to the natural rhythm of the changing relationship between the sun and the earth. So the solstices and the equinoxes are marked by celebrations to promote the advent of new birth after the shortest day in winter and to welcome its fulfilment in the spring; to give thanks for the long days of the summer and for the fruits of the autumn. Many religious festivals follow these cycles with appropriate action for spiritual support to maintain the well being of the community.

Nowadays the original impetus of these celebrations can be blurred by the dominance of commercialisation, so it is good to realise how much our aspirations and rejoicings still depend on Mother Nature. Besides the traditional celebrations I have included a number of action days or weeks on conservation, which have a much more recent origin. These too can take the form of festivals, celebrating our love and concern for all the earth's treasures that are under threat. In both kinds of celebration there can be special attention paid to activities that are in harmony with nature and the need for conservation.

Sometimes the traditional approach can be adapted to ecological action: children might give a dramatic presentation of a Mummers' play dealing with endangered species – an elephant instead of a bear! On St George's Day the dragon could be threatened with extinction or it could be a threat to the environment. I have tried to make a few suggestions on these lines and for creative activities to strengthen the original ties with nature, but not to impose any pressure which might spoil the fun. As well as the well-loved traditional festivities, action days or weeks can also be enjoyable and stimulating for children. Some of the older ones might like to write to their MP's or the United Nations and even quite young ones can pen a protest about the whales or the rain forests and they are much more likely to get a hearing! The organisations that have a children's section as described in the last chapter will be building the foundations in young people for a greater awareness of what can be done.

Emphasis on both the traditional festivals and pressure group action draws in the wider community, which is a step in the right direction; as the present trend has been for families, both urban and rural, to become more and more isolated. If children do put on a show or go on a sponsored action on some conservation issue, it is likely to be well received, as there is a growing consciousness concerning the state of the planet. It need not be a doleful affair, with awesome warnings; children will see to it that there are laughs and entertainment even if it is a serious campaign.

A number of the old festivals have a tradition of money being collected from house to house by children dressed up in disguise or bringing offerings. Rather than beg for candles on Candlemas Day, which is really out of date, could they collect for some conservation cause?

The idea throughout this book is that by being in touch with the natural world the children will eventually want to protect it; so pressure is at a minimum. If they grow up to be actively creative in enjoying the festivals, they have the basis for expressing their feelings and they will make up their own minds as to what they want to do in the future.

A Green Calendar of Festivals Old and New

January 1st Why not make a New Year's resolution to look after the environment in some of the ways suggested in this book!

Hogmanay   The Scots celebrate the New Year with great gusto and then 'first footing' begins: the first person to enter your house after midnight, bringing bread, coal and salt, will bring you luck and you will not be poor, cold or hungry in the coming year. Could this be a time when we contribute to those who are hungry and homeless?

February 2nd – Candlemas Day   A festival of the blessings of candles. Hibernating animals, and in particular the badger are supposed to wake up and see if it is still winter. Snowdrops planted in the autumn should be in bloom now and they will come up year after year in the garden or a large container, always spreading, so that you can dig some up to give away in decorated pots. This is a day to make your own candles (see page 81). In the old days children would go from house to house begging for candles and goodies – now they might sell their candles for a good cause!

Feb 2nd Candlemas

February 14th – St Valentine's Day   In folklore this is the day when the birds choose their mates, so celebrate with the birds by giving them a treat of food or a new bath. Children could make valentine biscuits in the shape of a heart and design valentine cards in the Victorian style with silver paper, lace, velvet, satin and pressed ferns.

Feb 14th St Valentine's day

Tuesday before Lent – Shrove Tuesday   Pancakes were made to use up the eggs and butter before Lent and they are still tossed in homes all over the country on Shrove Tuesday. Would it be a good idea for more communities to revive the exciting custom of the pancake race, as at Olney in Buckinghamshire; but this time with children participating? A 'pancake bell' is rung half an hour, then a quarter of an hour, before the race is due to start. At the word 'Go!' the participants toss their pancakes and once again during the run and then at the finish. There could be a pancake picnic, as the bell should have released children from school for the dinner hour!

Tuesday before Lent – Shrove Tuesday

March 1st – St David's Day   Wear a daffodil (or a leek). If your name is David have a name day celebration. This might be an inspiration to have name days as well as birthdays as in many countries. Children can find out when their name day occurs and if there isn't one they can choose one that appeals to them.

March 17th – St Patrick's Day   You don't have to be Irish to sport a shamrock or a sprig of clover. Boys named Patrick and girls named Patricia will be specially feted.

4th Sunday in Lent – Mothering Sunday   This is the day when young girls in service were allowed to visit their family. They usually baked a simnel cake with eleven, (for the apostles except Judas) marzipan balls on the top for their mothers. Children could make marzipan sweets with nuts pressed on them to give to their mothers or a plant that they have grown in a pot.

4th Sunday in Lent – Mothering Sunday

Between March 21st and April 25th – Easter Sunday

Eggs are always part of Easter celebrations: they can be boiled in various vegetable waters to obtain different colours: onion skins wrapped and tied round the eggs give a dappled orange effect; beetroot water makes them pink and spinach green. The custom of pace-egging is being revived when children soot their faces and go round knocking at doors asking for Easter eggs. Today if they collected money for some conservation issue they would get a good response. Treasure hunts and egg-rolling down hills are still popular, especially when the eggs have been colourfully decorated beforehand.

Between March 21st and April 25th (Easter Sunday)

April 23rd – St George's Day   Children could make up a play about St George and the Dragon – perhaps with the dragon ruining the countryside! Cowslips were picked and made into balls to decorate the house in the old days; now they are a protected species, so the best way to celebrate would be to buy a packet of wild cowslip seeds and plant them first in pots and then on the roadside or on some wasteland.

May 1st – May Day   Although it is already a 'threatened species', the next Monday after May 1st is now a national holiday as in the old days and the maypole is coming back into its own, with a pole instead of a felled tree. May baskets can be made from recycled containers such as strawberry boxes and decorated with greenery or a flower plant in a pot and given to neighbours.

May 1st – May Day

Full Moon in May or June – Wesak Day   Buddhists celebrate the life of the Buddha on Wesak Day and set free caged birds or animals to symbolise warm feelings for every living creature. Children can take special care of animals and make Wesak lanterns out of citrus fruit skins as illustrated.

Full Moon in May or June – Wesak Day

22nd–31st May – Environment Week   This is a nationwide event with hundreds of organisations participating at grass roots level to protect the environment.

May 29th – Oak-Apple Day   This is a celebration of King Charles II's restoration to the throne after hiding from his enemies in an oak tree. As 'pagan' festivities such as May Day had been forbidden, these became linked with Oak Apple Day when a sprig of oak is worn and children dressed up as Green Men (and women nowadays!) This costume can be simply made with green material in the form of a tube gathered at the neck with arm holes cut out and leaves stuck or sewn all over it. A crown of leaves completes the effect, as illustrated, all ready for a green picnic!

May 29th – Oak-Apple Day

29th May–5th June – National Bat Week   This is a countrywide effort to protect bats, which are now a threatened species. Bat boxes can provide welcome shelter as many of their habitats have been taken over or destroyed, or are treated with toxic preservatives, which they cannot tolerate.

June 5th – World Environment Day   This is a day to draw attention to the alarming state of the environment worldwide: letters to the press and to international organisations on the increasing pollution and threat to so many species would be appropriate.

14th–18th June – Endangered Species Day   This follows on from World Environment Day and families might choose their particular endangered species to press for its survival; it might be orchids or whales, otters or rhinos.

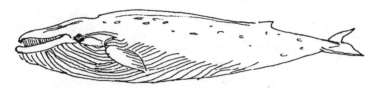

June 5th – World Environment Day (blue whale)

June 21st – Midsummer's Eve   This is a magic time and often celebrated with bonfires, which people used to leap over to change their luck. The Druids have always gathered at Stonehenge to watch the sunrise after the solstice and this celebration appeals to many people who would like to celebrate this heartfelt custom.

19th–27th June – Green Transport Week   This week focuses on the need to cut down on car travel, by walking, cycling (and pressing for cycle lanes), having a rota of car travel, switching to unleaded petrol and even to a catalytic converter. Their immediate objectives are: reducing car mileage by 20 per cent; taking a bus or train for one in every five journeys; making at least one two-mile trip by bicycle; walking at least two journeys that would otherwise be made by car; writing three letters – to the local MP and the leaders of the district and county councils, asking each to use their powers to green the transport network locally and nationally. Walking to school can be surprisingly stimulating for young children.

13th–17th September – Tidy Travel Week   This calls for a concerted approach against all kinds of litter especially in places of recreation and leisure such as the seashore.

13th–17th September – Tidy Travel Week

September – Harvest Festivals These festivals are celebrated the world over to give thanks for crops safely harvested. The ceremony of the corn dolly was concerned with the idea of preserving the corn spirit. The last sheaf was used to make an elaborate corn dolly, which was then planted in the first new furrow the following spring on Plough Monday to ensure a good harvest. A much simpler corn (corn on the cob) dolly can be made.

September 3rd – Nutting Day This was a favourite day for searching for hazel nuts and see if one could find 'fivers', 'sixers' or even 'seveners'! This date has probably become too early since the change in the calendar, perhaps the nuts would be more likely to be ripe on the 21st September, the Devil's Nutting Day, when it was forbidden! This should not deter families to go nutting at anytime during September and making some nut biscuits or nut loaves.

September 3rd – Nutting Day

The Last Sunday in September – Forbidden Britain Day
This is your opportunity to join the Ramblers Association to let the Government know that you want access to our open country, which is being increasingly closed to the general public.

The Last Sunday in September – Forbidden Britain Day

Before October 10th – Blackberry Days   The 10th is supposed to be Devil's Blackberry Day, so it is important to choose a day before then!

14th–20th October – Wildlife Week   This is the time to plan a wildlife garden or to join in pressure groups to protect endangered wildlife.

21st October – Apple Day   The aim is to plant and promote a variety of apples grown locally. Apple Day was only formed in 1991 and is well on the way to becoming a national celebration with apple fairs and picnics, tastings and especially apple tree planting. It has already become established in many schools and is an enjoyable focus for community celebrations.

27th October–3rd November – National Dormouse Week It is sad to think that there is a danger of the dormouse becoming rare to the point of extinction. We can make safe habitats of brushwood and grass in our wildlife patches to entice them to make their homes there.

27th October-3rd November – National Dormouse Week

Last Thursday in October – Punkie Night   Children go from house to house with lanterns of mangolds, (or today swedes and turnips) cut out with elaborate designs, to ask for money.

The New Moon in Late October or Early November – Divali   This is the Hindu festival of lights when small lamps or candles are placed in all doorways and windows. Children can make the traditional pottery oil lamps, known as divas.

October 31st – Halloween   The children dress up and disguise themselves and carry pumpkin or turnip lanterns from house to house. Previously it was a question of neighbours guessing who they were, today the American practice of trick or treat has been introduced and parents need to be confident that their children will not overstep the mark on the 'trick' side. A washable chalk mark on the door is acceptable but not a paint spray!

October 31st – Halloween

November 5th – Guy Fawkes Day   Many neighbourhoods are making this a community affair, rather than each family celebrating individually, with shared fireworks and bonfires, both for safety and environmental reasons.

25th November-5th December – National Tree Week   This is a well established action week to protect and plant trees: there is publicity and protest over the destruction of the rain forests and tree planting ceremonies throughout the country. The Woodland Trust works all year round to conserve and sustain our rapidly disappearing woods and concentrates on National Tree Week to plant trees and draw attention to the need for a concerted campaign, together with 'Men of the trees' and many other environmental groups.

Four Sundays before Christmas – Advent Sunday   Make an Advent ring which is usually a wreath of evergreens with four candles attached to it firmly with wire. One candle is lit for a while on Advent Sunday and another on the next Sunday and so on until the fourth Sunday; then on Christmas Eve all four candles are lit together. Some families make matchbox chests of drawers, each containing a tiny treasure and they open one every day until Christmas.

Four Sundays before Christmas – Advent Sunday

December 25th – Christmas   There is such feasting at Christmas that it is good to give to others at this time. It could be contributing to the homeless in some way – and not just for Christmas. The children could give the birds a feast decorating a tree branch with necklaces of peanuts, suet cones and dried fruit 'cakes'. Make sure that your Christmas tree has its roots and that they have not been scalded; then you can keep it outside in the garden or a container to use next year.

December 26th–1st January – The Week of the Christmas Walk   This week is jointly organised by the Rambler's Association and the National Trust with the special purpose of walking and clearing the public footpaths so that they will not be closed owing to disuse. This is the practice of the Rambler's Association throughout the year and families are especially welcome.

Appendix
A Selection of Environmental Organisations in Britain

ACID RAIN
INFORMATION CENTRE
Dept of Environmental &
Geographical Studies
Manchester Polytechnic
Chester Street Manchester
M1 5GD

ALUCAN
Suite 308
1 Mex House
52 Blucher Street
Birmingham
B1 1QU

ANIMAL AID
7 Castle Street
Tonbridge
Kent
TN9 1BH

ARK TRUST
498–500 Harrow Road
London
W9 3QA

THE ASSOCIATION FOR
THE PROTECTION OF
RURAL SCOTLAND (APRS)
14a Napier Road
Edinburgh
EH10 5AY

BRITISH BUTTERFLY
CONSERVATION SOCIETY
Tudor House
Quorn
Loughborough
Leicestershire
LE12 8AD

BRITISH HEDGEHOG
PRESERVATION SOCIETY
Knowbury House
Knowbury
Shropshire

BRITISH NATURALISTS'
ASSOCIATION
48 Russell Way
Higham Ferrers
Northants
NN9 8EJ

BRITISH UNION FOR THE
ABOLITION OF
VIVISECTION
16a Crane Grove
London
N7 8LB

CAMPAIGN FOR
NUCLEAR
DISARMAMENT
162 Holloway Road
London
N7 8DQ

THE CENTRE FOR
ALTERNATIVE
TECHNOLOGY
Machynlleth
Powys
Wales
SY20 9AZ

CHICKEN'S LIB
PO Box 2
Holmfirth
Huddersfield
West Yorkshire
HD7 1QT

CHILDREN'S SCRAPSTORE
The Federation of Resource
Centres
Greater Manchester Play
Resource Unit
Grumpy House
Vaughan Street
West Gorton
Manchester
M12 5DU

COMMON GROUND
45 Shelton Street
London
WC2H 9HJ

COMMONWORK
Bore Place
Chiddingstone
Edenbridge
Kent
TN8 7AR

COMMUNITY RECYCLING
OPPORTUNITIES
PROGRAMME (CROP)
7 Colts Holm Road
Old Wolverton
Milton Keynes
MK12 5QD

COMPASSION IN WORLD
FARMING
Charles House
5A Charles Street
Petersfield
Hampshire
GU32 3EH

COUNCIL FOR
ENVIRONMENTAL
EDUCATION
School of Education
University of Reading
Berks
RG1 5AQ

COUNCIL FOR
PROTECTION OF RURAL
ENGLAND (CPRE)
Warwick House
25 Buckingham Palace Road
London
SW1W OPP

COUNTRYSIDE
COMMISSION
John Dower House
Crescent Place
Cheltenham
Gloucestershire
GL50 3RA

COUNTRYSIDE COUNCIL
FOR WALES
Plas Penrhos
Ffordd Penrhos
Bangor
Gwyneth
LL57 2LQ

CYCLISTS TOURING CLUB
69 Meadrow
Godalming
Surrey
GU7 3HS

ENGLISH NATURE
Northminster House
Peterborough
PE1 1UA

ENVIRONMENTAL
INVESTIGATION AGENCY
2 Pear Tree Court
London
EC1R 0DS

FORESTS SCHOOL CAMPS
110 Burbage Road
London
SE24 9HD
FRIENDS OF THE EARTH
26 Underwood Street
London
N1 7JQ

GREEN PARTY
10 Station Parade
Balham High Road
London
SW12 9AZ

GREENPEACE
Greenpeace House
Canonbury Villas
London
N1 2PN

GREEN TEACHER
Llys Awel
22 Heol Pentrerhedyn
Machynlleth
Powys
North Wales

INTERMEDIATE
TECHNOLOGY
DEVELOPMENT GROUP
103 Southampton Row
London
WC1

INTERNATIONAL
COUNCIL FOR BIRD
PRESERVATION
32 Cambridge Road
Girton
Cambridge
CB3 OPJ

INTERNATIONAL FUND
FOR ANIMAL WELFARE
(IFAW)
Tubwell House
New Road
Crowborough
East Sussex
TN6 2QH

INTERNATIONAL
SOCIETY FOR
PREVENTION OF WATER
POLLUTION
Little Orchard
Bentworth
Alton
Hampshire
GU34 5RB

JERSEY WILDLIFE
PRESERVATION TRUST
Les Augres Manor
Trinity
Jersey
Channel Islands

KEEP BRITAIN TIDY
GROUP
Bostel House
37 West Street
Brighton
BN1 2RE

LEAGUE AGAINST CRUEL
SPORTS
Sparling House
83-87 Union Street
London
SE1 1SG

LIVING EARTH
FOUNDATION
The Old Laundry
Ossington Buildings
Moxon Street
London
W1M 3JD

MAMMAL SOCIETY
Dept. of Zoology
University of Bristol
Woodland Road
Bristol
BS8 1UG

MARINE CONSERVATION
SOCIETY
9 Gloucester Road
Ross-on-Wye
Herefordshire
HR9 5BU

MEN OF TREES
Sandy Lane
Crawley Down
Crawley
West Sussex
RH10 4HL

NATIONAL COUNCIL FOR
VOLUNTARY
ORGANISATIONS
Regents Wharf
8 All Saints Street
London
N1 9RL

NATIONAL FEDERATION
OF CITY FARMS
AMF House
93 Whitby Road
Brislington
Bristol
BS4 3QF

NATIONAL SOCIETY FOR
CLEAN AIR
136 North Street
Brighton
East Sussex
BN1 1RG

NATIONAL TRUST
36 Queen Anne's Gate
London
SW1H 9AS

NATURE CONSERVANCY
COUNCIL FOR SCOTLAND
12 Hope Terrace
Edinburgh
EH9 2AS

OXFAM
274 Banbury Road
Oxford
OX2 7DZ

PEDESTRIANS
ASSOCIATION
126 Aldersgate Street
London
EC1 4JQ

PLAY FOR LIFE
31b Ipswich Road
Norwich
NR2 2LN

RAMBLERS ASSOCIATION
1-5 Wandsworth Road
London
SW8 2XX

ROYAL SOCIETY FOR
NATURE CONSERVATION
The Green
Witham Park
Lincolnshire
LN5 7JR

ROYAL SOCIETY FOR THE
PREVENTION OF
ACCIDENTS
Cannon House
The Priory
Queensway
Birmingham
B4 6BS

ROYAL SOCIETY FOR THE
PREVENTION OF
CRUELTY TO ANIMALS
(RSPCA)
Causeway
Horsham
West Sussex
RH12 1HG

ROYAL SOCIETY FOR THE
PROTECTION OF BIRDS
(RSPB)
The Lodge
Sandy
Bedfordshire
SG19 2DL

SCOTTISH WILDLIFE
TRUST
Cramond House
Kirk Cramond
Cramond Glebe Road
Edinburgh
EH4 6NS

SOIL ASSOCIATION
86-88 Colston Street
Bristol
Avon
BS1 5BB

SURVIVAL
INTERNATIONAL
310 Edgware Road
London
W2 1DY

THAMES WATER
AUTHORITY
Rivers Division
Nugent House
Vastern Road
Reading
Berkshire
RG1 8DB

TIDY BRITAIN GROUP
The Pier
Wigan
WN3 4EX

TRANSPORT 2000
Walkden House
10 Melton Street
London
NW1 2EJ

UNIVERSITIES
FEDERATION FOR
ANIMAL WELFARE
(UFAW)
8 Hamilton Close
South Mimms
Potters Bar
Hertfordshire
EN6 3QD

URBAN SPACE SCHEME
(USS)
Department of Food and
Biological Sciences
Polytechnic of North London
Holloway Road
London
N5

URBAN WILDLIFE GROUP
(UWG)
Unit 310
Jubilee Trade Centre
130 Pershore Street
Birmingham
B5 6ND

VEGETARIAN SOCIETY
Park Dale Road
Altringham
Cheshire
WA14 4QG

WARMER CAMPAIGN
83 Mount Ephraim
Tunbridge Wells
Kent
TN4 8BS

WASTE WATCH
68 Grafton Way
London
W1P 5LE

WATCH TRUST FOR
ENVIRONMENTAL
EDUCATION
22 The Green
Nettleham
Lincoln
LN2 2NR

WATER AUTHORITIES
ASSOCIATION
1 Queen Annes Gate
London
SW1H 9BT

WHALE AND DOLPHIN
CONSERVATION SOCIETY
PO Box 981
Bath
Avon
BA1 2BT

WILDFOWL AND
WETLANDS TRUST
The Wildfowl and Wetlands
Centre
Slimbridge
Gloucestershire
GL2 7BT

WOMEN'S
ENVIRONMENTAL
NETWORK
Aberdeen Studios
22 Highbury Grove
London
N5 2EA

WOODCRAFT FOLK
13 Ritherdon Road
London
SW17 8QE

WOODLAND TRUST
Autumn Park
Dysart Road
Grantham
Lincolnshire
NG31 6LL

WORKING WEEKENDS ON
ORGANIC FARMS
19 Bradford Road
Lewes
Sussex
BN7 1RB

WORLD WIDE FUND FOR
NATURE (WWF)
Panda House
Weyside Park
Godlaming
Surrey
GU7 1XR

YOUNG
ARCHAEOLOGISTS CLUB
Bowes Morrell House
Walmgate
York
Y01

YOUNG PEOPLE'S TRUST
FOR ENDANGERED
SPECIES
19 Quarry Street
Guildford
Surrey
GU1 3EH

YOUNG PEOPLE'S TRUST
FOR THE ENVIRONMENT
AND NATURE
CONSERVATION
9 Leapale Road
Guildford
Surrey
GU1 4JX

YOUTH HOSTELS
ASSOCIATION
Trevelyan House
8 St Stephen's Hill
St Albans
Hertfordshire
AL1 2DY

YOUTH TAG
TECHNOLOGY ACTION
GROUP (YT)
Myson House
Railway Terrace
Rugby
CV21 3HT

ZOO CHECK
Cherry Tree Cottage
Coldharbour
Dorking
Surrey
RH5 6HA

Also by Mildred Masheder:

LET'S PLAY TOGETHER

An exciting collection of over 300 games and sports which put co-operation before competition – and make everyone a winner!

Each game is coded to indicate at a glance the age groups most likely to enjoy it. People with disabilities can take part too: suitable games are specially marked.

And there's no problem with numbers: the minimum number of players for each game is clearly shown – so choosing games is easy whether for just a couple of people or a big party, and lots of the games can be played in teams.

You'll find traditional party games, circle games, games for the lively and energetic, and parachute games. There are a number of co-operative sports, and a selection of games from around the world.

Playing games will never be the same again.

ISBN 1 85425 013 2

Pbk £6.99

Green Print
10 Malden Road
London
NW5 3HR